DrawPlus X5 User Guide

How to Contact Us

Our main office
(UK, Europe):

The Software Centre
PO Box 2000, Nottingham,
NG11 7GW, UK

Main: (0115) 914 2000

Registration (UK only): (0800) 376 1989

Sales (UK only): (0800) 376 7070

Customer Service/
Technical Support: http://www.support.serif.com/

General Fax: (0115) 914 2020

North American office
(USA, Canada):

The Software Center,
17 Hampshire Drive, Suites 1& 2,
Hudson, NH 03051, USA

Main: (603) 889-8650

Registration: (800) 794-6876

Sales: (800) 55-SERIF or 557-3743

Customer Service/
Technical Support: http://www.support.serif.com/

General Fax: (603) 889-1127

Online

Visit us on the web at: http://www.serif.com/

International

Please contact your local distributor/dealer. For further details, please contact us
at one of our phone numbers above.

Credits

This User Guide, and the software described in it, is furnished under an end user License Agreement, which is included with the product. The agreement specifies the permitted and prohibited uses.

Trademarks

DrawPlus is a registered trademark of Serif (Europe) Ltd.

All Serif product names are trademarks of Serif (Europe) Ltd.

Microsoft, Windows, and the Windows logo are registered trademarks of Microsoft Corporation. All other trademarks acknowledged.

Windows Vista and the Windows Vista Start button are trademarks or registered trademarks of Microsoft Corporation in the United States and/or other countries.

Adobe Flash is a registered trademark of Adobe Systems Incorporated in the United States and/or other countries.

Wacom, the logo and Intuos are trademarks or registered trademarks of the Wacom Company, Ltd.

Copyrights

Digital Images © 2008 Hemera Technologies Inc. All Rights Reserved.

Digital Images © 2008 Jupiterimages Corporation, All Rights Reserved.

Digital Images © 2008 Jupiterimages France SAS, All Rights Reserved.

Bitstream Font content © 1981-2005 Bitstream Inc. All rights reserved.

Portions graphics import/export technology © LEAD Technologies, Inc. & Eastman Kodak Company.

Panose Typeface Matching System © 1991, 1992, 1995-1997 Hewlett-Packard Corporation.

The Sentry Spelling-Checker Engine © 2000 Wintertree Software Inc.

PANTONE* Colors displayed in the software application or in the user documentation may not match PANTONE-identified standards. Consult current PANTONE Color Publications for accurate color. PANTONE* and other Pantone, Inc. trademarks are the property of Pantone, Inc. © Pantone, Inc., 2005.

Pantone, Inc. is the copyright owner of color data and/or software which are licensed to Serif (Europe) Ltd. to distribute for use only in combination with DrawPlus. PANTONE Color Data and/or Software shall not be copied onto another disk or into memory unless as part of the execution of DrawPlus.

FontForge © 2000,2001,2002,2003,2004,2005,2006,2007,2008 by George Williams.

Portions of this software are copyright © 2008 The FreeType Project (www.freetype.org). All rights reserved.

Contents

11. Creating Animations......................................223

12. Publishing and Sharing 253

13. Pressure sensitivity and pen tablets.............273

14. Index 283

1 Welcome

Welcome to **DrawPlus X5**—the design and illustration solution from **Serif**, packed with all the features expected of award-winning design software. From **decorative page elements** and **logos** to **full-page illustrations**, **scale drawings**, **multi-page folded publications**, and **Stopframe** or **Keyframe animations**— DrawPlus X5 does it all. With the power of scalable vector graphics at your command, you'll see the creative possibilities open up right before your eyes! Whether you're a beginner or an expert, you'll find easy-to-use tools you can use right away.

If you've upgraded from a previous version, this new edition of DrawPlus includes a host of exciting new features (see p. 12) which complement DrawPlus's existing features listed overleaf. We hope you also enjoy the additional power and performance edge.

Don't forget to register your new copy, using the **Registration Wizard** on the **Help** menu. That way, we can keep you informed of new developments and future upgrades!

Existing features

As you might expect from powerful design software, DrawPlus is packed with a comprehensive range of design tools and options in an easy-to-use user environment.

Document

- **Multipage Document Support**
  From startup to printout, the versatile DrawPlus engine sustains your creativity. Choose from a wide range of preset document types, including booklets and folded documents. Work on pages right side up... **automatic imposition** assures correct order and orientation of your output.

- **Import PDF**
  Unlock the contents of third-party PDF drawings using DrawPlus's impressive "open PDF" feature—objects can be brought into a new drawing with a single-click for immediate editing.

- **Layers**
  Each page can have multiple layers so you can assign elements to different layers for modular design. Each layer entry hosts a hierarchical tree view of associated thumbnailed objects.

- **Pseudo 3D Projections**
  Project objects isometrically onto Top, Front, or Right planes via a Standard toolbar. For more advanced projections, take advantage of editable Dimetric, Trimetric, Oblique projections, or even create your own Custom projection.

- **View Quality**
  Draw in different drawing modes to view objects at optimum quality (Normal mode) or unsmoothed (Draft).

- **Professional-Standard Drawing Features**
  Features like converting text to curves, defining custom envelopes, fully customizable drop shadows, layers, and scalable vector graphics give complete creative power. Combine two shapes into one... Subtract for cropping and masking... Intersect to carve out unique shapes and regions.

Illustration essentials

- **Rotate Canvas**
  Let your canvas rotate through any angle, just like an artist would do in real-life. Great for artists with tablets, for drawing freeform curves at any orientation, and for getting a different perspective of your drawing!

- **Pressure Studio for pen tablets**
  Calibrate and **test** your tablet's input devices, even setup **function keys**, **rings**, **wheels**, and **sliders** from within DrawPlus—all in one easy-to-use studio! For Wacom Intuos4 users, take advantage of OLED touch-sensitive shortcuts, where illuminated DrawPlus tool icons show in your tablet's Functions area.

- **Design aids**
  Use Overlays such as **Rule of Thirds** grid (for improved page composition) and **Divine Proportions** (for aesthetic proportioning).

For more focused design, use **Solo mode** to work on an object in isolation.

Ease of Use

- **Tailor your keyboard shortcuts**
  Take advantage of customizable keyboard shortcuts for enhanced productivity—assign your own keystrokes to toolbar and menu commands! Use single-key keyboard shortcuts for easy tool access.

- **Snapping power for fine positioning**
  Align objects relative to nearby objects by using colour-coded **dynamic guides; vertex snapping** lets you snap to an object's natural corners and points. Great for engineering drawing, flow charting, and general precision layout. An in-built candidate system for snapping to objects "in focus" is used.

Design

- **Cropping**
  Any object can serve as a "cookie cutter" for trimming one or more other objects into a single shape... and the effect is reversible so you won't lose your originals. Great for creating "reflections" of complex scenes!

- **Vector editing tools**
  Tools such as Knife Tool cuts through objects, leaving them in multiple parts, still as vectors. The Erase Tool removes areas under a brush line of variable nib width to redefine object boundaries! The opposite of the Erase Tool, the Freeform Paint Tool "adds to" current vector objects (shapes, text, bitmaps).

- **Comprehensive Design Gallery**
  The Gallery tab provides an impressive selection of instantly available Arts & Crafts, Cartoons, ShapeArt, Connecting Symbols (family trees, electronics, computers), and Layout Symbols (garden and interior design), and many more. Use the Gallery to additionally store and organize your own favourite designs for future use!

- **Picture Import and Adjustments**
  Import pictures from hard disk, CD/DVD, PhotoCD, digital camera or scanner. Use image adjustments for quick fixes (or special effects)

including Red Eye Tool, Auto Levels, Auto Contrast, Brightness/Contrast, and many more. Apply adjustments singularly or in combination. Use PhotoLab for studio-based adjustments, effects, retouching, and masking.

- **Object Default control**
  Set your intended object's default line colour/style, fill, and transparency before even drawing your object! As a more powerful default control, Synchronize Defaults lets you adopt a currently selected object's attributes for future objects. for example, select a red brush stroke to subsequently paint in red, then a green brush stroke to paint in green. All or selected attributes can be affected. Global and object-specific defaults can be reset independently.

- **Resource Management**
  Swap out your already placed bitmaps or text fragments in Drawing mode or any Animation mode from the new Media tab; a Keyframe animation's movie or audio clip can also be replaced.

Colour and Transparency

- **Design Power with Colour Gradient Fills**
  The Gradient Fill Editor allows you to adjust gradient contour and tint any portion of the colour spread, locate key colours precisely... and select from RGB, HSL, CMYK, PANTONE® or Registration colours via a Colour Selector.

- **Advanced Fill Support**
  Simply apply solid colours from the Studio's Colour tab or Swatch tab onto a fill path to add or replace colours for more subtle gradients. Choose colours from different colour mixing modes in the Colour tab—HSL Wheel (and other models) offer different ways to mix colour. Load RGB, CMYK and coordinated "themed" palettes from within the Swatch tab. Apply high-end linear, radial, conical, ellipse, three colour, four colour, square, and plasma fills to any text or shape for exciting, professional results. Use bitmap fills for textures and backgrounds. Add, view, edit, or delete colours used in your current drawing from within a saveable Document Palette. Even import your own bitmaps and use them as fills on DrawPlus objects! Plus Mesh Fills for impressively varied gradients using a path-node network.

Define new colour sets based on a base colour—this linkage can transform the drawing's colour scheme instantly, by simply modifying that base colour!

- **Colour Picker Tool**
  Sample colours directly under the cursor or, for artefacted, halftone or dithered images, by **averaging colours** under a shaped region. Don't forget to try **colour gradient** sampling, for sampling sunsets, metal or glass surfaces, and more.

- **Colour Palette Designer**
  Create your own palettes from **colour spreads** based on accepted colour theory (**Monochromatic**, **Complementary**, **Triadic**, and more). You can add suggested colours automatically, or mix your own colours to create the new palette. Spreads are perfect for simulating various **skin** and **natural tones**.

- **Opacity control in Colour tab**
  For improved productivity, any colour chosen in DrawPlus can now have an associated **Opacity** applied at the same time. Great for setting colour/opacity combinations on objects or nodes on fill paths!

- **Transparency Effects**
  Transparency can make the difference between flat, ordinary visuals and sparkling realism! And DrawPlus provides it all—a full range of transparencies for shading, shadows, reflections, depth effects, and more.

Lines, brushes, and shapes

- **Versatile Freeform Line Drawing**
  Sketch cartoons and line art using the Pencil Tool. Pressure sensitivity is supported on **freeform lines**, with weight and opacity control. Add rounded corners when and where you need them... and choose different end caps and joins. Create decorative chain lines for marching footprints, themed borders, and much more.

- **Natural Curve Editing**
  Simply click and drag to break and redraw a curve at any node. Apply smoothing selectively to freeform curves to eliminate that "shaky hand" appearance.

- **Dimension Lines and Scale Setting**
  Click a couple of times to take linear or angular measurements of any object on the page—DrawPlus displays the dimension using your choice of ruler units, at your specified scale (say, one inch to two feet). Dimensions update when objects are moved or resized! Design room layouts, make maps, draw scale models, and more.

- **Connectors**
  For drawing dynamic flow diagrams, schematics, family trees, and organization charts, connectors let you link your boxes and symbols and then rearrange at will. Connection points stay put on each object... keeping connections intact. Auto Connectors intelligently display bridges at line crossings, and even route themselves around obstructive objects. Perfect in combination with the Gallery tab's exciting range of **office flow chart symbols** or with ever dependable QuickShapes.

- **Intelligent Curve Tracing**
  Simply "connect the dots" to trace around curved objects and pictures... the Pen Tool features Smart segments that use automatic curve-fitting to connect each node!

- **Brushes**
  Unleash the painter within you, with DrawPlus's powerful Paintbrush Tool and the supporting Brush tab's galleries! Pick from natural media brush types such as acrylic, charcoal, dry paint, pastel, pen, and watercolour, or create your own. Use brush-specific pressure properties—especially good for natural brush textures. **Recolour** photo brushes in an instant! Using a pressure-sensitive pen tablet? Pressure sensitivity is supported (via a Pressure tab) with preset or custom pressure profiles and control over the maximum and minimum pressure applied.

- **QuickShapes**
  QuickShapes work like intelligent clipart… or the most powerful set of drawing tools you've ever envisaged. Even extremely complex shapes like spirals, stars, and webs are simple to draw and customize using QuickShapes. Type text directly into any shape!

Text

- **Working with Text**
  Apply and edit artistic, frame, or shape text right on the page... apply basic formatting from the always-at-hand Text context toolbar. Control advanced properties like text flow (wrap), kerning, leading, paragraph indents, above/below spacing. Need foreign language support? Simply paste text in Unicode format as either formatted RTF or unformatted plain text. Font substitutions during the opening of DrawPlus or PDF files offers an interactive means of managing missing fonts. Use Spell Checker to proof your output—check any text against an editable user dictionary.

- **Add text to a path easily**
  Make your text fit to any line and shape's outline easily—simply draw then type text directly on the object's path.

Pictures

- **AutoTrace**
  Convert pictures to vector art with AutoTrace Studio. Adopt **preset profiles** for tracing logos, as well as colour and black-and-white photos. Create your own **custom profiles** for tracing files with similar characteristics. Use **adjustment tools** for fine-tuning traced output (add/remove colours and edit curves).

- **Quick-and-easy Image Cutouts**
  Image Cutout Studio makes light work of cutting out your placed pictures and images, directly within DrawPlus. Use brushes to discard uniform backgrounds (sky, walls, etc.) or keep subjects of interest (people, objects, etc.).

Effects

- **Perform Powerful Blends**
  The Blend Tool allows adjustment of blend steps, transform, and attribute profiles (rate of change). Objects can be multiply-blended (to/from other blends) to create truly stunning illustrations.

- **Instant 3D with on-screen transforms**
  Transform 3D objects with in-situ 3D rotational control and editing. Apply awesome multi-coloured lighting effects (with directional control), along with custom bevel and lathe effect profiles to create your very own unique contours. Hardware-accelerated rendering boosts redraw performance (hardware dependent).

- **Perspective Effects**
  Get a new slant on things... With a context toolbar flyout full of presets plus a built-in tool for freeform adjustments, the Perspective Tool lets you tilt and skew text (or any other object) for truly "spatial" results!

- **Roughen Tool**
  For jagged, jaunty edges on text, lines, or QuickShapes, just drag the tool up or down for subtle or bold results.

- **Border Wizard**
  Vastly flexible Border Wizard instantly adds borders to the page or to individual objects. Choose a border from the extensive library, or be creative and let Border Wizard guide you through building a unique design.

- **Filter Effects**
  Drop shadows starting to wear a bit thin? Enliven your text with fully adjustable Inner Shadow, Glow, Bevel, and Emboss filters... easy to apply and sure to impress. Apply soft edges with the Feathering filter effect—great for blends, montages, vignetted photo borders, and much more.

- **Astounding 3D Lighting and Surface Effects**
  Advanced algorithms bring flat shapes to life! Choose one or more effects, then vary surface and source light properties. Adjust parameters for incredible surface contours, textures, fills. The Studio's Styles tab offers preset 3D effects you can apply and customize as you wish.

Web and Animation

- **Web Image Slices, Image Maps, Rollover States**
  Beat the pros at their own game by using these techniques to add links to your Web graphics! With a few clicks, divide images into segments—each with its own hyperlink and popup text—or add hotspots to specific regions. Even let DrawPlus create interactive rollover Web graphics that highlight or change state when users mouse over or click!

- **Stopframe Animation**
  Tap the power of QuickShapes to turn out Web stopframe animations in no time—using advanced features like onion skinning, backgrounds, overlays, and frame management.

- **Keyframe Animation**
  Produce smooth, professional and quick-to-design animations as Adobe® Flash® files, all from within the Storyboard tab. The Easing tab defines editable envelope profiles for defining the rate of change of an object's transformation and attributes. The Actions tab can assign "events" (mouse click, hover over, and many more) and an associated action (e.g., jump to a named URL or animation marker); develop directly in ActionScript for the more adventurous! Use the Keyframe Camera to pan, zoom, or rotate around your animation's keyframes. Add sound and movies to any Keyframe animation. Export to Flash, Flash Lite/i-Mode, screensaver or a choice of video formats.

Export and Print

- **Image Export**
  Image Export lets you see how your image will look (and how much space it will take up) before you save it! Its multi-window display provides side-by-side WYSIWYG previews of image quality at various output settings, so you can make the best choice every time. Take advantage of super sampling for superior quality export. Use Dynamic Preview to work in an edit-and-preview mode at a given DPI, file format, and number of colours.

- **PDF Export**
  Step up to the worldwide standard for cross-platform, WYSIWYG electronic information delivery. Your PDF output will look just like your DrawPlus document... in one compact package with embeddable fonts, easily printable or viewable in a Web browser.

- **Professional Print Output**
  PDF publishing to the PDF/X-1 or PDF/X-1a file format is a great choice for professional output from DrawPlus. Deliver with confidence to your print partner, safe in the knowledge that your single composite print-ready PDF drawing includes all fonts and colour information for spot or process colour separation. Select file information, crop marks, registration targets, and densitometer/colour calibration bars for inclusion in your PDF. You have full control over prepress settings for output.

New features

Professional

- **New Architecture—Better Performance!**
  With a new drawing engine, DrawPlus is now faster, more powerful, and optimized for computers with multi-core processors. Enjoy even greater drawing fidelity!

- **Start-to-Finish CMYK Workflow** (see p. 23)
  For professional printing to PDF or image, create drawings in CMYK primary colour mode! You'll be able to work natively in CMYK colour space, right through to pre-press output. **Live Plate View** lets you interactively switch on/off CMYK plates as you draw.

- **Composite Opacity and Knockout Groups** (see p. 169)
  Assign opacity to a group, along with grouped objects, using **composite opacity**! As another opacity control, **knockout groups** prevent overlapped, semi-transparent object areas from contributing their opacity to overlapping objects.

- **Composite Blend Modes and Isolated Blending** (see p. 165)
  Like composite opacity, a composite blend mode affects a group, after overlapping grouped objects are blended. For control of blending scope, **isolated blending** restricts blending effects to just the group (and not underlying objects).

- **Accurate Ruler Guide Placement** (see p. 39)
  Use **Guides Manager** to create and accurately position multiple ruler guides. Manage guides in bulk, either on the current page or across a folded document spread.

- **Document-level Colour Management**
  Assign different ICC profiles to each RGB or CMYK drawing.

Creative

- **Powerful Targeted Drawing** (see p. 50)
  Draw In Front, **Behind**, or **Inside** any targeted object. All absolutely essential when working with complex arrangements of overlapping objects. Drawing inside restricts drawing to within the object's outline.

- **Add Shapes Together for Complex Art** (see p. 130)
  The **Shape Builder Tool** makes light work of creating wild and abstract shapes from smaller shapes! Simply drag and join shapes, subtract areas, or create areas (including intersections).

- **Blending on a Path** (see p. 202)
  Make any blended object follow any previously drawn curve—great for decorative contouring and spirals.

- **Professional-level OpenType Font Features** (see p. 104)
  For embellished text, DrawPlus fully utilizes all your OpenType font features—**ligatures**, **stylistic sets/alternates**, **small/petite caps**, **case-sensitive forms**, **fractions**, **ordinals** are available.

- **Ready-to-use Graphic Styles—Fantastic Effects!** (see p. 86)
  The **Styles tab** lets you choose from various preset **shadows**, **glows**, **bevels**, **feather edges**, **textures**, **text effects**, and more. A graphic style, when applied, complements an object's existing graphic styles. For **custom** design, save your own **graphic styles** with control over which object properties (and attributes) are stored!

Ease of Use

- **Customized Menus and Toolbars**
  Tailor DrawPlus to your needs with **menu**, **toolbar**, and **icon customization**.

- **Dynamic Reordering of Objects** (see p. 138)
  Drag the Arrange tab's **Depth** slider to dynamically change the selected object's order in the current layer.

- **Enhanced Solo Mode** (see p. 54)
  For progressively detailed design work, use multi-level **Solo Mode**! You'll be able to focus on chosen areas in isolation, using a select-then-solo approach—previous view levels can be returned to if needed. Operations are restricted to the current solo level, with the Layers tab only showing the objects currently in view!

Text

- **Proofing Tools as You Type** (see p. 112)
  Auto-Correct and **Underline spelling mistakes as you type** proofing options are at hand.

Printing and Sharing

- **Interactive Print Preview with print-time imposition** (see p. 259)
  Try out the exciting new **Print Preview**, packed with both preview and imposition options—create **books**, **booklets**, **thumbnails**, and **tiled** print output all **without prior page setup**.

- **Easier than ever Printing!** (see p. 253)
  Try DrawPlus's **Print** dialog for the options you need, when you need them! With a focus on everyday printing options, including **scaling** of your print output, the printing process becomes more intuitive and logical.

and some improvements on previous versions of DrawPlus...

- **Importing lots of pictures**? Select multiple pictures, import, then place on the page from a handy **Picture List** window.

- The **Pen** Tool becomes even more powerful with intelligent smart curve drawing, now complementing Bézier and Straight line drawing.

- Changing **fonts**? Use **live font preview** on any selected artistic or frame text.

- For accessibility, DrawPlus now offers two sets of **icon sizes**—Small and Large.

- Change the look of DrawPlus in an instant with exciting **Colour Schemes**.

- For professional web developers, **Dynamic Preview's pixel grid** is automatically enabled at higher zoom levels. Use with the snapping grid for pixel accurate object resizing and positioning!

Installation

System Requirements

Minimum:

- Pentium PC with DVD/CD drive and mouse

- Microsoft Windows® XP (32 bit), Windows® Vista, or Windows® 7 operating system

- 512MB RAM

- 820MB (recommended full install) free hard disk space

- 1024 x 768 monitor resolution

Additional disk resources and memory are required when editing large or complex documents.

> To enjoy the full benefit of brushes and their textures, you must be using a computer whose processor supports SSE (most modern computers do). On brush selection, an on-screen message will indicate if your computer is non-SSE.

Recommended:

As above but:

- Dual-processor PC technology

Optional:

- Windows-compatible printer

- TWAIN-compatible scanner and/or digital camera

- Pressure-sensitive pen tablet (Serif GraphicsPad or equivalent)

- 3D accelerated graphics card with DirectX 9 (or above) or OpenGL support

- Internet account and connection required for accessing online resources

First-time install

To install DrawPlus X5 simply insert the DrawPlus X5 Program CD into your DVD/CD drive. The AutoRun feature automatically starts the Setup process. Just answer the on-screen questions to install the program.

Re-install

To re-install the software or to change the installation at a later date, select **Control Panel** from the Windows Start menu and then click on the **Programs - Uninstall a program** option. Make sure the DrawPlus X5 Program CD is inserted into your DVD/CD drive, then select Serif DrawPlus X5, click the **Change** button and simply follow the on-screen instructions.

★ Use equivalent options for Windows XP.

2 Getting Started

Startup Wizard

Once DrawPlus has been installed, you're ready to start. Setup adds a **Serif DrawPlus X5** item to the **All Programs** submenu of the Windows **Start** menu.

- Use the Windows **Start** button to start DrawPlus (or if DrawPlus is already running, choose **New>New from Startup Wizard...** from the **File** menu) to display the Startup Wizard.

The Startup Wizard offers different routes into the program for you to explore:

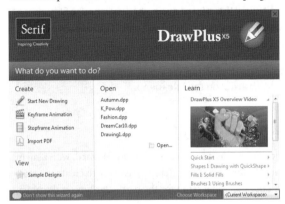

The above options are described as follows:

- **Start New Drawing**, to create a drawing from scratch.

- **Keyframe Animation**, to create a Keyframe animation.

- **Stopframe Animation**, to create a Stopframe animation.

- **Import PDF**, to create a design from an existing PDF file.

- **Sample Designs**, to load some example drawing files to boost your imagination!

- **Open**, to access recently opened drawings. Hover over each entry for a quick preview!

- **Learn**, to access online tutorials, support information, and more.

Use the **Choose Workspace** drop-down menu to choose your workspace appearance (i.e., Studio tab positions, tab sizes, and show/hide tab status). You can adopt the default workspace profile <**Default Profile**>, the last used profile <**Current Profile**>, a range of profile presets, or a workspace profile you've previously saved.

> 💡 As you click on different profiles from the menu, your workspace will preview each tab layout in turn.

The Startup Wizard is displayed by default when you launch DrawPlus. You can switch it off via the **Don't show this wizard again** check box on the Startup Wizard screen, or on again via **Startup Wizard** in **Tools>Options...** (use User Interface>Ease of Use menu option).

> 📌 You can also access the Startup Wizard at any time from **New>New from Startup Wizard...** on the **File** menu.

Starting with a new drawing

The first time you launch DrawPlus, you'll see the **Startup Wizard**, with a menu of choices. The **Start New Drawing** option offers an easy way to create your new drawing and lets you choose the initial setup for the particular type of document you'll be producing.

During **Page Setup**, DrawPlus offers a wide range of preset document types from several categories:

Category	Document types
Regular	Portrait or landscape in all the commonly encountered page sizes.
Folded	Greeting cards, menus, and tri- or Z-fold booklets.

Large

Banners, posters

Small

Labels, business cards, tags

Technical Drawing

ISO and ANSI layouts

> 🐾 For folded documents, automatic imposition assures correct order and orientation of your output.

To start a new drawing from scratch using the Startup Wizard:

1. Start DrawPlus (or choose **File>New>New from Startup Wizard...** if it's already running).

2. Select **Start New Drawing** from the Startup Wizard.

3. From **Page Setup**, review document categories in the left-hand pane (and sub-categories if applicable). Categories contain preset document types (see above) or if you select **Regular**, you can choose from standard document sizes presented in Portrait or Landscape sub-categories.

4.   Select a document type thumbnail from a category in the left-hand pane.

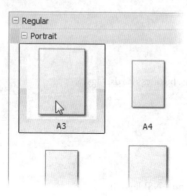

5.   (Optional) For custom settings, from the right-hand of the dialog, click a **Paper**, **Folding**, or **Margins** setting and either choose a different drop-down list option or input new values to modify. Typically, you can change paper Width, Height, and Orientation settings in the **Paper** category.

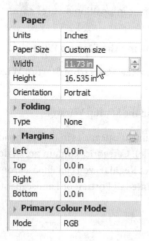

6.   (Optional) Set your colour mode to either RGB or CMYK (below) from the **Primary Colour Mode** section. CMYK is used for professional printing. For more details, see Working in RGB or CMYK colour mode below.

7.   Click **OK**. The new document opens.

To start a new drawing during your DrawPlus session:

●   Click  **New Drawing** on the **Standard** toolbar (if Startup Wizard is disabled).

- or -

Choose **New>New Drawing** from the **File** menu.

You'll get a new drawing in a new window each time you choose this method—the most recent page size and orientation chosen previously is used.

> ✱   You can always adjust the page settings later via **File>Page Setup...**.
>
> ✱   To start with a new keyframe or stopframe animation, see Getting started with animation on p. 223.
>
> ☿   Use Import PDF from the **Startup Wizard** to unlock the contents of third-party PDF drawings.

Working in RGB or CMYK colour mode

Whichever document type you choose, you'll be able to begin your design in either RGB or CMYK colour modes. The former is suitable when creating graphics for the web; the latter is ideal for professional pre-press PDF or image output (see p. 262 or p. 263, respectively). At any point in the future, you can change from RGB to CMYK, or CMYK to RGB modes easily.

Working in a specific workflow (RGB or CMYK) means that objects are drawn natively using the currently set colour space, without the needed for conversion to alternative colour spaces (e.g., from RGB to CMYK).

In CMYK mode, you can choose to show or hide each of the C, M, Y, or K plates while drawing by using the View tab.

 You can check which colour mode you are operating in, by viewing the Title Bar. This reports the document name followed by the document's current colour mode, e.g. [Drawing1.dpp (CMYK)].

Opening a saved document

You can open an existing DrawPlus drawing from the Startup Wizard, **Standard** toolbar or the **File** menu. Once a drawing is opened in its own document window, the window (and drawing) can be made currently active from a Document tab or via the **Window** menu.

To open an existing document from the Startup Wizard:

1. From the Startup Wizard (at startup time or via **File>New>New From Startup Wizard**), review your drawings in the **Open** section. The most recently opened file will be shown at the top of the list. To see a thumbnail preview of any file before opening, hover over its name in the list.

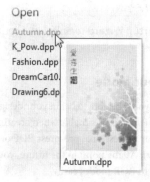

2. Click the file name to open it.

- If your drawing hasn't been opened recently, click ⬜ **Browse...** to navigate to it.

- Recently viewed files also appear at the bottom of the **File** menu. Simply select the file name to open it.

To open an existing document via toolbar or menu:

1. Click 📂 **Open** on the **Standard** toolbar, or select **File>Open...**.

2. In the Open dialog, navigate to, then select the file name and click the **Open** button.

Displaying drawings

Click on a Document tab at the top of the workspace to make it active. Active drawings are promoted to the front of the tabs (e.g., "Lorem3.dpp"). Unsaved drawings are indicated by an asterisk.

```
1 Lorem1.dpp *
2 Lorem2.dpp
✓ 3 Lorem3.dpp *
```

Alternatively, jump between drawings by selecting the drawing's window name from the **Window** menu. Asterisks indicate unsaved documents in the window; the currently active window is shown with a tick.

Opening other file types

Opening images as a new document

DrawPlus allows a comprehensive range of image file formats to be opened, each as a separate DrawPlus document. From the document, you can add your own text captions, lines, shapes, or apply image adjustments and effects (see p. 188). You can save your design changes as a new project or just export the image (with or without adjustment), while preserving its original properties.

To open an image:

1. Click   **Open** on the **Standard** toolbar.

2. Change the file type drop-down menu to display **All Image Files**, locate and select the file, and click **Open**. The image occupies your workspace such that page dimensions are adjusted to match the image dimensions (a **Custom** page size is adopted; in pixels).

3. (Optional) You can modify the image—modify the document as for any other document or double-click the image to load PhotoLab (then apply one or more effects or adjustments).

4. Click   **Save** to save the document as a DrawPlus .dpp project, or **File>Export>Export as Image...** to export it to the same or a different file format (the original image's name, dpi, colour depth, and transparency settings are maintained for export).

Importing PDF

It is possible to import PDF files—once opened, you can save your page content as a DrawPlus Drawing (.dpp). The character formatting, layout and images in the original PDF document are preserved to allow for editing of the imported content.

For PDF import, any fonts used in the original PDF document but not available on your computer can be substituted for suitable replacement fonts of your choosing. This is possible during the import process via a PDF Import Options dialog.

To import a PDF:

1. From the Startup Wizard, select **Import PDF**.

2. Navigate to, then select the name of the file, and click **Open**.

3. From the dialog, you can perform font substitution, choose text control options, import individual or all pages in the PDF file, and auto crop to the PDF page area.

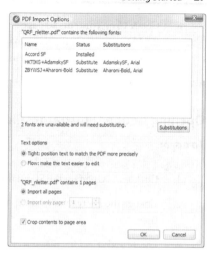

- The font list shows the fonts which are needed to represent the imported PDF text accurately and their current status, i.e.

Font Status	The font is...
Installed	installed on your computer.
Substitute	not installed on your computer so a suggested substitute font is selected for you. Instead, to use a different substituted font, click the **Substitutions** button. See Font substitutions in DrawPlus Help.

4. Choose a Text option, where **Tight** attempts to preserve the physical position of text in the original PDF (by preventing text wrapping), while **Flow** makes text editing easier, but at the expense of original text accuracy (by allowing text to wrap, making paragraphs from lines, and applying list formatting).

5. Enable **Import only page** to choose an individual PDF page to import. Otherwise, all PDF pages will be imported.

6.   Check **Crop contents to page area** to remove unwanted areas outside the PDF page such as printer marks (crop marks, registration targets, colour bars) or additional text instructions.

7.   Click **OK**.

Opening Adobe® Illustrator® files

To open:

1.   Click ⬚ **Open** on the **Standard** toolbar.

2.   Change the file type drop-down menu to display **Adobe Illustrator files (*.ai)**.

3.   Locate and select the file, and click **Open**.

> ✎ You can only open Adobe Illustrator files of Version 9 or above, which have also been saved within Adobe Illustrator as being PDF compatible.

Opening vector graphic files

DrawPlus can open a range of vector graphic files, including:

- **Serif Metafile** (SMF). This is a proprietary Serif format, intended to be used between Serif applications (e.g., WebPlus/PagePlus to DrawPlus) to retain graphic fidelity without loss of quality.

- **Scalable Vector Graphics** (SVG). This is an all-purpose format, ideal for sharing between vector applications. They can be uncompressed (.svg) or compressed (.svgz).

To open:

1.   Click ⬚ **Open** on the **Standard** toolbar.

2.   Change the file type drop-down menu to display **Serif Metafile Format (*.smf)** or **Scalable Vector Format (*.svg, *.svgz)**.

3.   Locate and select the file, and click **Open**.

Opening AutoCAD files

DrawPlus opens AutoCAD® .dwg and .dxf files quickly and easily. Using the same process as that for PDF files, this creates an opportunity to not only view engineering layouts and designs (up to AutoCAD 2006) in DrawPlus, but to edit the drawn objects and to save the drawing as a DrawPlus drawing (.dpp).

On file open, a **DXF/DWG Options** dialog provides options to scale the imported file objects, position the artwork on the page and merge objects onto one layer.

To open an AutoCAD file:

1. Click 📋 **Open** on the **Standard** toolbar.

2. Change the file type drop-down menu to display **AutoCAD files** (***.dwg,*.dxf**), locate and select the file, and click **Open**.

3. In the dialog, specify scaling and positioning options. Uncheck **Merge Layers** to retain the layer structure of the original AutoCAD file—layers will automatically be shown in the Layers tab.

4. Click **OK**. The AutoCAD drawing is imported.

Saving your work

DrawPlus saves its documents as .dpp (Drawing), .dpx (Template) or .dpa (Animation) files (for Stopframe and Keyframe animation modes).

To save your work:

- Click 💾 **Save** on the **Standard** toolbar.
  - or -
  To save the document under its current name, choose **Save...** from the **File** menu.
  - or -
  To save under a different name, choose **Save As...** from the **File** menu.

Closing DrawPlus

To close the current document:

- Click ✕ on the active document tab.

If the document is still unsaved or there are unsaved changes, you'll be prompted to save changes.

To close DrawPlus:

- Choose **Exit** from the **File** menu.

For each open window, you'll be prompted to save any changes made since the last save.

Updating defaults

When you create new objects in DrawPlus, the way they look depends on the current default settings for that particular type of object. DrawPlus stores defaults separately for (1) lines/shapes (including connectors and QuickShapes), (2) brushes, (3) artistic/frame text, (4) 3D filter effects, and (5) dimension lines.

Defaults for shape text (as contained in shapes) are distinct from those for artistic/frame text, and are defined along with other shape defaults (they are subsumed under other shape properties). For any object, default means the properties of the object that will be applied to the next new object (of the same type) you create.

You can adopt two approaches to controlling your defaults according to your preferred way of working, i.e.

 Synchronize Defaults (from flyout on **Standard** toolbar)	**On**	Defaults are changed **dynamically** by synchronizing to the colour, style, transparency, or effect of the currently selected item (or tab setting). For example, when painting, you might want to reuse the colour of a previously painted brush stroke. This is the default mode of operation.

Synchronize Defaults	**Off**	Defaults are changed by **manually** updating to the current item selection, and apply until they are manually updated again.

Normally, fill and line colours, line styles, and line/brush transparency will adopt the former approach. Brush strokes take a line colour, so they also synchronize to the currently set colour. Text attributes and filter effect defaults adopt the latter approach.

> To see what the current defaults are for a particular object type, simply create a new object of that type.

Although you can switch Synchronize Defaults on or off globally, it is also possible to independently switch on or off attributes which synchronize with, or update to, the currently selected object.

To change which attributes synchronize:

1. Choose **Synchronization Settings...** from the 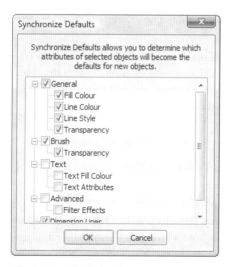 **Defaults** flyout (**Standard** toolbar) to optionally select attributes (e.g., fill colour, line colour, transparency, etc) from which new defaults will be made.

2. Check or uncheck the check boxes to switch on or off the synchronization of defaults for that attribute.

To switch synchronize defaults off (for manual default control):

- Uncheck **Synchronize Defaults** on the 🌐 ▾ **Defaults** flyout of the **Standard** toolbar.

To set object defaults manually:

1. With **Synchronize Defaults** disabled, create a sample object (the object type matching the set of defaults you're updating, and alter it to use the specific properties you plan to use as defaults.
   - or -
   Use an existing object that already has the right properties.

2. Right-click the object and choose **Update Defaults** (or choose **Update Object Defaults** from the **Format** menu).

🔖 When you update defaults from a shape, all default shape properties, including **shape text** attributes, are reset at the same time.

🔖 Shape text properties are stored along with other shape defaults, such as line and fill. To avoid altering these settings when updating shape text defaults, create a new sample shape and modify only its text.

Normally, each time you close a document, object default settings are recorded as "master settings" to be used in future documents. To stop DrawPlus from recording the defaults as master settings, choose **Tools>Save Settings...** and uncheck the **Object Defaults** box.

Resetting defaults

A reset of defaults is useful if you feel the need to get back to basics and return to your original default settings.

- Select **Reset Object Defaults** from the 🌐 ▾ **Defaults** flyout (**Standard** toolbar). With no objects selected, this acts globally, i.e., it resets all objects back to their default settings. With an object(s) selected, it resets only those object types back to their default.

3   Working with Pages

Using the page and pasteboard

Most of the DrawPlus display is taken up by a **page** or "artwork" area and a surrounding **pasteboard** area. This arrangement is an electronic equivalent of the system used by traditional graphic designers. They kept design tools and bits of text and graphics on a large pasteboard, and then carefully pasted final arrangements of text and graphics onto a page-sized "artwork" sheet pinned down in the middle of the board.

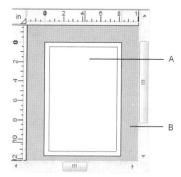

(A) Page and (B) Pasteboard

The **page area** is where you put the text and graphic elements that you want to be part of the final output. The **pasteboard area** is where you generally keep any elements that are being prepared or waiting to be positioned on the page area.

Setting measurement units and drawing scale

For precision drawing, you need techniques that allow you to position and draw accurately without effort, that will also be of use at any scaled size. Such techniques make use of rulers and guides for actual-size or scaled drawings.

Rulers

The DrawPlus rulers mimic the paste-up artist's T-square, and acts as a measuring tool and guide creator. The rulers that surround the page allow you to measure the exact position of an object.

Ruler units used by DrawPlus determine the units displayed on the rulers and the reported units shown when positioning and scaling objects (either around the object or on the **Hintline**). You can change the ruler units without altering the document's dimensions. Unit settings are saved with your DrawPlus document; as a result loading different documents, templates, etc. may change your working measurement units.

To change the page unit:

- Right-click on a ruler and select an alternative measurement unit.

> Ruler Units are equivalent to Page Units unless you're working on a scale drawing. For example, at 100% zoom, one ruler centimetre equals one centimetre on the printed page.

Moving rulers

By default, the horizontal ruler lies along the top of the DrawPlus window and the vertical ruler along the left edge. The default **ruler intersection** is the top-left corner of the pasteboard area. The default **zero point** (marked as 0 on each ruler) is the top-left corner of the page area.

To move either ruler to a different position, click and drag on the ruler intersection button (showing the type of measurement unit).

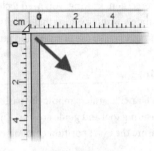

To set a new **ruler origin**—simply drag the ⊿ tab onto the page and release to set the position of your new origin (cross-hair guides and the **Hintline** toolbar help this positioning). Double-click on the intersection to reset the origin back to its default position. All guide positions are recalculated as the origin changes position.

Double-click on the ruler intersection to make the rulers' zero point jump to the top left-hand corner of the selected object.

This comes in handy for measuring page objects. If the rulers have already been moved or the object is deselected, double-clicking on the intersection will send the rulers back to the default position.

Rulers as a measuring tool

The most obvious role for rulers is as a measuring tool. As you move the mouse pointer, a small line marker along each ruler displays the current horizontal and vertical cursor position. When you select an object the rulers not only show its position, but also its extent by a lighter coloured area (also showing the object's dimensions).

Creating guides

If you want to position objects repeatedly on the same horizontal or vertical boundary then **guides** can be used. DrawPlus lets you set up horizontal and vertical **guides**—non-printing, red lines you can use to align one object with another. Guides are "sticky" as long as you have **Snap to Guides** turned on (via **Tools>Options**; Layout>Snapping), i.e., a moved object will behave as if it is attracted to a guide as you move it close to the line. Guides also attract the object when you are changing its size.

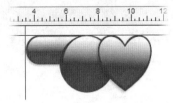

Guides can be created (and positioned) either by dragging from a ruler or via the **Guides Manager**. Both methods let you add guides to the current page, or, if creating a folded document, guides across a page spread.

To create a guide (by dragging):

- For a horizontal or vertical guide, click on the horizontal or vertical ruler, respectively, and drag onto the page while fine-tuning the guide into its position.

> Hold down the **Alt** key before guide creation to produce a horizontal guide from a vertical ruler and vice versa.

To **move** a guide, click and drag it into position with the Pointer Tool. To **remove** a guide, drag and drop it onto the respective ruler.

Alternatively, the Guides Manager lets you precisely create, edit, or delete ruler guides via a dialog.

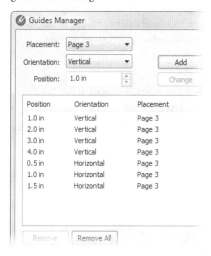

To create a guide (via Guides Manager):

1. Right-click a ruler and select **Guides Manager...**.

2. From the dialog, select a **Placement** (the current page or folded document's Spread) and **Orientation**.

3. Enter a **Position** value. This is the ruler position where you want to place the guide.

4. Click **Add**.

5. Repeat for other guides.

6. Click **OK**.

Use **Remove** or **Remove All** to delete a selected guide, or all guides, respectively.

To show/hide or lock guides:

*   To **show** or **hide** guides, check or uncheck **Layout Tools>Guides** from the **View** menu (or use **Tools>Options**; Layout>Grid and Guides).

*   To **lock** the guides and prevent them from being moved, right-click on a ruler and select **Lock Guides**.

Drawing scale

You can create **scale drawings** (such as a garden design or model diagram) by setting a ratio other than 1:1 between page units and ruler units. For example, you might wish to set one page centimetre equivalent to 0.5 metre, a good scaling ratio for designing gardens of a typical size.

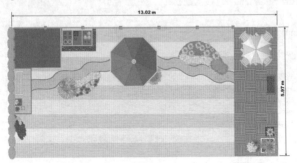

Use Dimension tools (see p. 82) in conjunction with scale drawings for on-the-page measurements, which automatically update as you move objects.

To change the drawing scale:

1. Choose 📐 **Drawing Scale Options** from the context toolbar (shown with Pointer or Rotate Tool selected).
   - or -
   Choose **Options...** from the **Tools** menu and select the Layout>Drawing Scale option.

2. Check the **Scale Drawing** box.

3. Use the input boxes to set the drawing scale as a proportion between the Page Distance (in **page units** that define the document's actual printing dimensions) and the Ruler Distance (in on-screen **ruler units** that represent the "real world" objects you're depicting). Units and object dimensions update and scale accordingly.

For clarity, the dialog also reports the **Printed page size** (in page units, as shown in the Page Setup dialog) and the **Scaled page size** (in "real world" ruler units).

When creating graphics for the computer screen, as opposed to the printed page, it's useful to set a drawing scale ratio of one inch (Page Distance) to 96 pixels (Ruler Distance).

Using snapping

The **Snapping** feature simplifies placement and alignment by "magnetizing" moved or resized objects to various page layout aids and elements. Aids include guide lines and snapping grid, while elements include page margins, rows, columns, page edge, and page/margin centres.

Dynamic guides can be used to align and resize objects to existing object edges, centres, and vertices. Guides appear automatically as you drag objects. For technical/engineering drawing use, dynamic guides further support snapping to object vertices (e.g., the points of a star, shape nodes and line/curve nodes). See Using dynamic guides on p. 38.

To turn snapping on and off globally:

- Click **Snapping** on the **Standard** toolbar., check or uncheck the **Snapping** box.

Alternatively, switch **Snapping** on or off via the **Arrange** menu.

To turn individual snapping controls on and off:

- Click the down arrow on the **Snapping** button (**Standard** toolbar) and check/uncheck a specific snapping option via the drop-down list (e.g., Snap to Guides).

All snapping options are described as follows:

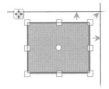

Snap to Guides
Objects will jump to visible ruler guides.

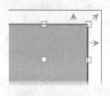

Snap to Margin

Objects will jump to align with defined page margins.

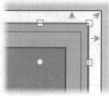

Snap to Page Edge

Objects will jump to the absolute page edge.

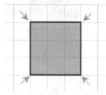

Snap to Grid

Objects will jump to align with a visible grid's dots, lines or dashes.

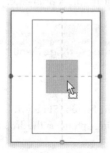

Snap to Margin Centres

Objects jump to margin centres (i.e., the centre of the page in relation to the page margins).

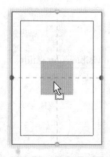

Snap to Page Centre

Objects jump to the page centre (i.e., the centre of the page in relation to the page edge).

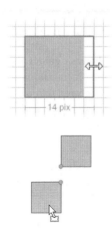

Snap to Units

Objects will jump to snapping measurement units, independent of ruler measurement units. For example, a shape can be resized by pixel on a supporting pixel grid.

Use dynamic guides

A moved object can be aligned precisely with an already placed object, using optional vertex snapping.

See Using dynamic guides on p. 44 for more details.

Using the snapping grid

The **Snapping Grid**, when enabled, appears as a matrix of dots, lines or dashes covering the page. It's especially useful as an alignment aid on the page when Snap to Grid (see above) is also enabled.

To show or hide the snapping grid:

- From the **Standard** toolbar, click [image] **Overlays** and select **Snapping Grid** from the drop-down list. A grid is overlaid over your page.

  - or -

  Choose **Layout Tools** from the **View** menu and check or uncheck on the submenu.

  - or -

  Choose **Options...** from the **Tools** menu, select Layout>Grid and Guides, then check or uncheck the **Display Grid** box.

Snapping with dynamic guides

For accurate object alignment and resizing, you can use **dynamic guides** instead of either setting ruler guides manually or performing selection, transform, and alignment operations. These guides automatically display between the object being moved and the object to be aligned to, "visually suggesting" possible snapping options, and allow snapping to the object's left, right, centre, top, right, bottom, page centre, or vertices.

In technical/engineering drawing, dynamic guides are especially useful when snapping to object vertices, i.e., the natural points and corners of irregularly-shaped objects, lines/curves, and rotated bitmaps.

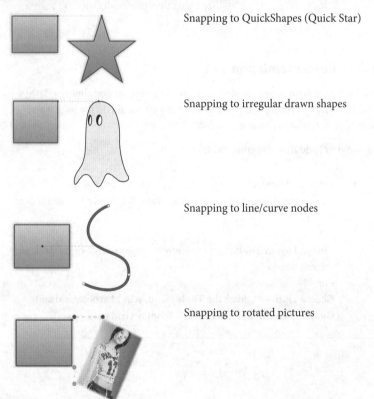

Snapping to QuickShapes (Quick Star)

Snapping to irregular drawn shapes

Snapping to line/curve nodes

Snapping to rotated pictures

For ease of use, dynamic guides always use a candidate system where objects previously selected, hovered over, or newly created become the focus for snapping. All other objects can't be snapped to until they are "activated"; the last several "activated" objects are included in each snapping operation.

If snapping to vertices isn't needed, perhaps during less technical design, you can switch the option off. Dynamic guides can also be switched off entirely if required.

To disable dynamic guides and snapping to vertices:

1. Click the down arrow on the  **Snapping** button (**Standard** toolbar) and select **Options...**.

2. From the dialog, uncheck **Dynamic guides** or just **Snap to Vertex**.

> To temporarily disable dynamic snapping, hold down the **Alt** key while moving an object for alignment.

Viewing pages

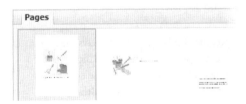

The HintLine toolbar at the bottom of the screen displays the current page number and provides a number of controls to let you navigate around your pages.

As an alternative, the Pages tab shows your pages as thumbnails, which when selected, will display that page in your workspace.

Once you've got a page in view, you can use the scrollbars at the right and bottom of the main window to move the page and pasteboard with respect to the main window. As you drag objects to the edge of the screen the scroll bars adjust automatically as the object is kept in view.

To go to a specific page:

1. Click ⬛ **Add/Delete Pages** on the HintLine toolbar.

2. On the Page Manager's **Go to Page** tab, select the page number to go from the drop-down list and click **OK**.

- or -

1. Display the **Pages tab** (docked at the bottom of your DrawPlus workspace) by clicking the ▬▬▲▬▬ button.

2. Click on a thumbnail to jump directly to that page.

> For folded documents such as greeting cards, the "inner" page spread will show as "Pages 2,3". When the thumbnail is selected, the page spread is shown in your workspace.

To navigate pages:

- Click ◀ **Previous page,** ▶ **Next page,** ⏮ **First page** or ⏭ **Last page** on the HintLine toolbar.

Zooming

The **Hintline** toolbar also allows the user to view and/or edit the page at different levels of detail. You can zoom in/out step-by-step or by a user-defined/preset amount. Panning is also possible.

75% The **Current Zoom** setting on the Hintline toolbar displays the current zoom percentage, with 100% representing an actual-size page. Click over the value, then type to enter any zoom percentage up to 5000% or select a preset zoom from the flyout list (includes fit to **Full Page** or **Page Width**).

To zoom to a particular view:

- Click ⊖ **Zoom Out** or ⊕ **Zoom In** to decrease/increase the current zoom percentage with each click.

- Click **Zoom Tool** and drag out a rectangular marquee on the page to define a region to zoom in to. To zoom out, hold down the **Shift** key when dragging or just right-click on the page. You can also pan around a zoomed-in page while the **Ctrl** key is pressed. To zoom to the current selection, choose **Selection** from the **View** menu.

- Click **Pan Tool** to use a hand cursor to click anywhere on the page and drag to reposition the page in the window.

- Click **Fit Page** to adjust the zoom percentage so the entire page area is displayed in the window.

If you're using a wheel mouse, you can scroll the wheel forward or back to move up or down the page, or move horizontally left or right by using the **Shift** key and scrolling together. Try combining the **Ctrl** key and scrolling up or down for immediate in/out zoom control.

View quality

DrawPlus can operate in two drawing view modes, each one offering a different view quality level, i.e., **Normal** and **Wireframe**. The respective modes offer decreasing view quality but will produce inversely greater drawing speeds. The difference between modes is especially noticeable on displayed bitmaps, filter effects, and brush strokes. By default, Normal mode is used for new documents and shows smoothing; Wireframe mode will show just an easily selectable single-pixel outline (without textured strokes, line widths, fills, and 2D/3D effects)—great for precision alignment and the ability to better manipulate overlapping object outlines.

> The Wireframe mode is a view mode only; objects in this view cannot be output to printer or exported as such.

To change view quality:

- Select **View Quality** from the **View** menu, then choose **Normal** or **Wireframe** from the menu.

Adding and deleting pages

DrawPlus lets you add one or more pages before or after a currently selected
page; you can even make use of an object "cloning" feature which copies objects
from a chosen page.

To add one or more new pages:

1.   Select a page from which to add page(s) before/after.

2.   Click ⊞ **Add/Delete Pages** on the HintLine toolbar.

3.   On the Page Manager's **Insert Page** tab, specify the following:

     ●   The number of pages to add

     ●   The page before (or after) the new pages should be added

     ●   Whether to duplicate a particular page by copying objects from it

4.   Click **OK**.

> 🖎   The document format (as determined in **File>Page Setup...**) will
> determine whether or not you can add or delete pages. For
> example, Folded documents have a fixed number of pages.

To delete one or more pages:

1.   On Page Manager's **Delete Page** tab, specify the following:

     ●   The number of pages to delete

     ●   The page after which pages should be deleted

2.   Click **OK**.

To duplicate a page:

●   On the Page Manager's **Insert Page** tab, you can specify how many
    pages to add, and where to add them. Check **Copy objects from page**
    if you want to duplicate a particular page.

To make a page a background for other pages:

- From the Pages tab, right-click the intended background page and choose **Set as Background** (to undo choose **Unset as background**). The page is named Background and is applied to other pages already present.

Anything you subsequently add to the background page will be replicated to other pages immediately.

Using design aids

DrawPlus provides a number of tools to assist you as you design. Each is designed to improve stroking lines/brushes, page composition, and focused design on specific areas on the page.

- Using drawing targets

- Rotating your canvas

- Applying the Rule of Thirds

- Using divine proportions

- Isolating an object

- Using multiple document windows

Using drawing targets

Drawing targets let you control how you draw in relation to a **selected** object.
The ability to draw **in front**, **behind**, or **inside** any currently selected object
provides an alternative to drawing objects that, by default, always appear in front
of all other layer objects. This extra control is of particular benefit on more
complex designs containing overlapping objects; the created object is placed
adjacent to (or clipped to) the originally selected object.

   Draw in Front   *Draw Behind*   *Draw Inside*

In the Layers tab, you'll see how objects created in front, behind, or inside the
currently selected object are placed above, below, or clipped to the selected
object. Objects at the top of the layer are displayed in front of object lower in the
layer.

To draw in front, behind, or inside the selected object:

1.   From the **Standard** toolbar, select a **Target**, i.e., **Draw
in Front**, **Draw Behind**, or **Draw Inside**.

2.   Draw over the selected object. You'll see the new object ordered
according to the Target chosen.

Rotating your canvas

Rotating your canvas helps you to maintain natural flow when drawing freeform lines, curves, or brush strokes, where the artist uses the wrist as a pivot (especially when using a pen tablet). If you rotate the canvas by a chosen angle then the drawing becomes easier—taking advantage of the natural arc of the drawing hand.

The above example illustrates how grass-like brush strokes can be added more easily to a canvas once it has been rotated 30°!

To rotate your canvas:

Either:

1. Click **Rotate Canvas** on the **Hintline** toolbar (don't click the down arrow).

2. Hover over your workspace until you see the cursor, then drag to rotate the canvas clockwise or anti-clockwise.

3. Once you're happy with the degree of rotation, release the mouse button to reposition the canvas.

- or -

- Click the down arrow on the **Rotate Canvas** button (**Hintline** toolbar) and choose a preset angle from the drop-down list.

❀ You can also select an object and then choose **To Object** from the
Rotate Canvas drop-down list. The canvas adjusts so that the
object is positioned square to the X and Y axes.

To reset your canvas:

● With the button enabled, double-click anywhere on the canvas to
reset.

Applying the Rule of Thirds

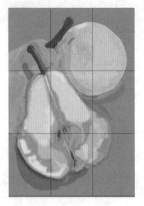

Traditionally a technique used in photography,
the **Rule of Thirds** grid can also be applied to your
design to help with its composition.

For example, note the way the primary object
(pear) is vertically aligned between the top- and
bottom-left intersecting points, i.e., under the stalk
and core. The secondary object (orange) is located
under the opposite intersecting line to offer some
balance to the design.

By aligning objects to intersecting horizontal and vertical lines (rather than just
centring objects on the page) you can create designs with greater visual interest.

When a grid is applied to your page the displayed context toolbar lets you alter
the grid's colour and opacity, and reset or delete the grid. (See DrawPlus Help.)

❀ The grid is actually an overlay which appears as an 'Overlay Layer' in
the Layers tab. As such you can use the ◉ **Visible** layer control to
temporarily show/hide the grid.

To apply a Rule of Thirds grid:

1. From the **Standard** toolbar, click 🖼️ ▾ **Overlays** and
select **Show/Hide Rule of Thirds** from the drop-down list. A coloured
grid is overlaid over your page.

2.   (Optional) For selected objects, drag a corner (or edge) handle to resize the grid or reposition the grid by dragging. The grid can be manipulated just like an object.

3.   Place pictures, frames, or vector objects under any of the intersecting blue lines.

Once applied, the grid stays selected. Clicking away from the grid will deselect it, but it can be reselected at any time (e.g., for repositioning later).

To select the grid:

-   From the **Standard** toolbar, click [icon] **Overlays** and choose **Select Rule of Thirds**.

Using divine proportions

Divine proportions in DrawPlus involve overlaying a grid over your design for aesthetic proportioning of design elements. The grid uses the classic golden ratio principle commonly encountered in:

-   classic drawings (e.g., da Vinci's Vitruvian Man).

-   musical instruments (opposite).

-   buildings (Athen's Parthenon).

-   modern iconic design (Apple iPod/iTouch).

> ✎   The golden ratio can be understood using a cello as an example— the ratio (0.618) is that between the instrument's neck and its body.

"Golden" Spirals, Rectangles, and Tangents make up the grid, each differently coloured for easy distinction. Their colours can be changed and each grid component can be hidden from the context toolbar.

To apply a Divine Proportions grid:

1. From the **Standard** toolbar, click  **Overlays** and select **Show/Hide Divine Proportions** from the drop-down menu. The grid is overlaid over your page.

2. (Optional) Resize, rotate, or reposition the grid over your design (or planned design area) by dragging corner or edge handles.

3. Begin drawing, using the guide lines to draw objects proportionately.

To select the grid (once deselected):

- From the **Standard** toolbar, click **Overlays** and choose **Select Divine Proportions**.

Isolating an object

For focused editing, DrawPlus X5 provides the **Solo mode**. This allows you to temporarily isolate selected object(s) on the page that you are currently designing (all unselected objects disappear!). In doing so, you avoid having to move objects to other layers or lock object unnecessarily.

DrawPlus supports **multi-level solo mode**, where you can further isolate sub-areas of your design within solo mode, allowing you to work in increasing levels of detail. This is carried out using a pop-up window, which hosts a **Solo** button which acts on currently selected page objects. The original drawing and each isolated level are shown as consecutive thumbnails.

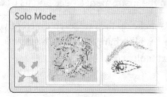

While in solo mode, the Layers tab will show only the objects present at the current solo level. This is ideal for managing objects at that level (especially selecting and ordering).

To isolate an object:

1. Select the object, then click **Solo Mode** on the **Hintline** toolbar.

2. Once in Solo mode, continue drawing in isolation.

The Solo Mode pop-up window shows the original drawing. If you want to optionally work on sub-areas of your "soloed" drawing, you can in work in multi-level solo mode.

3. Select object(s).

4. Click **Solo Mode**.

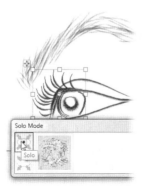

The selected object(s) is isolated for focused editing.

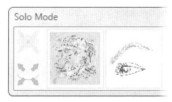

 Any edits you make are updated across all levels simultaneously.

To undo a solo level:

- Double-click a selected thumbnail or click ![icon] **Unsolo** in the Solo Mode window.

Using multiple document windows

Multiple document windows can be used effectively for comparing the same drawing, at different magnification levels. As you make fine adjustments to a specific area of your design in a new magnified window, you'll be able to use the original window to see how your changes look in the context of the whole drawing.

To create a new document window:

- Select **New Window** from the **Window** menu. The same drawing shows in a new window, e.g. "Drawing2 (RGB):2" where "2" represents the window number.

> ✦ You will need to position your windows and set your magnification level for side-by-side comparison.

4 Lines, Curves, and Shapes

Selecting one or more objects

Before you can change any object, you need to select it using one of several tools available from the top of the **Drawing** toolbar.

  Pointer Tool/Rotate Tool

From the Selection tool flyout, click the **Pointer Tool** to select, move, copy, resize, or rotate objects. Use the **Rotate Tool** to exclusively select and rotate an object around a centre of rotation. You can also use the Rotate Tool to move or copy objects.

 Node Tool

Click to use the **Node Tool** to manipulate the shape of objects, or move or copy objects.

To select an object:

- Click on the object using one of the tools shown above. For the Pointer and Rotate Tools, small "handles" appear around the object indicating selection.

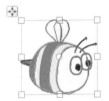

For the Node Tool, editable nodes are displayed for lines—sliding handles are additionally shown for adjustment of QuickShapes and text. If objects overlap, use the **Alt** key while clicking repeatedly until the desired item is selected.

When you draw an object it is initially selected for you so that you can modify it.

If you select an image with areas of transparency, you'll be able to manipulate the image's outline, i.e., convert to curves, apply line properties, effects.

Selecting multiple objects

It is also possible to select more than one object, making a **multiple selection** that you can manipulate as if it were one object, or turn into a grouped object (see p. 135).

To select more than one object (multiple selection):

1. Choose the **Pointer Tool** or **Rotate Tool**.

2. Click in a blank area of the page and drag a "marquee" box around the objects you want to select.

Release the mouse button. All of the objects within the marquee box are selected and one selection box, with handles, appears around the objects. To deselect, click in a blank area of the page.

- or -

1. Click on the first object for selection.

2. Press the **Shift** key down then click on a second object.

3. Continue selecting other objects to build up your multiple selection. Handles (or a bounding box, depending on the tool) appear around the multiple selection.

To select all objects on the page:

● Choose **Select All** from the **Edit** menu (or use **Ctrl+A**).

To add or remove an object from a multiple selection:

● Hold down the **Shift** key and click the object to be added or removed.

Selection using a lasso

For more detailed multiple object selection, using a fixed marquee or **Shift**-select may be too inflexible. Instead, you can draw an irregular-shaped lasso around one or more objects in a complex design.

To select using a lasso:

1. Choose the Pointer or Rotate Tool.

2. With the **Alt** key pressed, draw a "lasso" around the objects you want to select.

3. Release the mouse button. All of the objects within the lasso region are selected.

Drawing lines and shapes

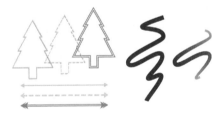

Lines can be either straight or curved, and can have properties like **colour** and **width** (thickness). They can also adopt specific **line styles**, **ends**, and **caps**.

Choose one of the line tools shown below from the **Drawing** toolbar.

 The **Pencil Tool** is used to sketch freeform lines.

 From the Line Tools flyout, the **Pen Tool** is used for drawing complex, combination curves and shapes in a highly controlled way by using a series of "connect the dots" mouse clicks. The **Straight Line Tool** is used to draw straight lines.

As soon as you draw a line, or choose one of the line tools when a line is selected, you'll see the line's **nodes** appear. Nodes show the end points of each segment in the line. Curved lines usually have many nodes; straight lines have only two.

If you're using a pen tablet or using simulated pressure sensitivity (with DrawPlus's Pressure tab), you'll be able to draw realistic lines of varying width and opacity using pressure sensitivity—just like drawing with real pencils and pens. See Pressure sensitivity on p. 275.

Drawing lines

To draw a freeform line:

1. Choose the  **Pencil Tool** from the **Drawing** toolbar.

2. Click once, then drag across the page, drawing a line as you go. The line appears immediately and follows your mouse movements.

3. To end the line, release the mouse button. The line will automatically smooth out using a minimal number of nodes. Note the little squares indicating its nodes—at the two ends, and at each point where two line segments come together.

4. (optional) To set the degree of smoothing to be applied to the line (and subsequent lines), set the **Smoothness** value on the context toolbar above your workspace.

Click its right arrow to display a slider—drag right, then left. You'll see your drawn line—still selected—smooth out (with fewer nodes) as you drag right, and become more jagged (with more nodes) as you drag left. For the smoothest curves the next time you draw a freeform line, leave the sliding arrow towards the right of the slider.

To draw a straight line:

1. 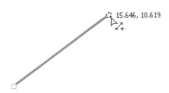 From the **Drawing** toolbar's Line Tools flyout, click the **Straight Line Tool**.

2. Click where you want the line to start, and drag to another point while holding down the mouse button, then release the mouse button. The straight line appears immediately.

> To constrain the angle of the straight line to 15° increments, hold down the **Shift** key down as you drag. (This is an easy way to make exactly vertical or horizontal lines.)

Any kind of open line (that is, one that hasn't been closed to create a shape) can be extended, and you can use any of the three line tools to do so. Use the Pointer Tool and then the line's drawing tool to resize or reshape lines once you've drawn them.

To extend a line:

1. Move the cursor over either of the end nodes (a small cursor will appear), and click the node.

2. The line that you drag out will be a continuation of the existing line, as a new line segment.

To draw a curved line:

1. Choose the **Pen Tool** from the **Drawing** toolbar's Line Tools flyout.

2. From the displayed context toolbar, choose to create your drawn segments in **Smooth**, **Smart**, or **Line Segments** creation **Mode**.

- **Smooth Segments**: draws Bézier curves smoothly segment-by-segment, with manual on-curve and off-curve adjustment via nodes and control handles, respectively.

- **Smart Segments** (default): automatically determines slope and depth for a rounded, best-fitting curve. No control handle adjustment is normally necessary.

- **Line Segments**: creates a zig-zag line without curving through nodes.

For Smart segments:

3. Ensure ⌃ **Smart Segments** is enabled.

4. Click and drag across your page to define the first smart segment (**1**).

5. For the next segment, position your cursor where you want the segment to end, and click (**2**).

6. Repeat for additional segments (**3**).

7. To end the line, press **Esc** or choose a different tool.

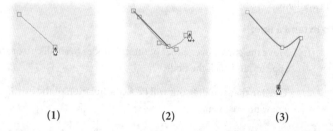

| (1) | (2) | (3) |

The square on-curve nodes created between segments have Smart corners by default, meaning that the corner intelligently curves automatically without adjustment.

For line segments:

3. Ensure ⌃ **Line Segments** is enabled.

4. Click and drag across your page to define the first smart segment (**1**).

5. For subsequent segments, position your cursor where you want the next segment to end, and click (**2**).

6. Repeat for additional segments (**3**).

7. To end the line, press **Esc** or choose a different tool.

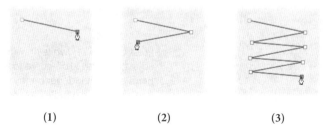

(**1**)   (**2**)   (**3**)

For smooth (Bézier) segments:

3. Ensure ⌢ **Smooth Segments** is enabled.

4. Click where you want the line to start (**1**).

5. Click again for a new node and drag out a pair of "off-curve" **control handles** which orbit the node and release the mouse button (**2**). (Control handles act like "magnets," pulling the curve into shape. The distance between handles determines the depth of the resulting curved line.) Normally, curve segments end in a smooth corner (**4**).

6. Repeat for additional segments (**3**).

7. To end the line, press **Esc** or choose a different tool.

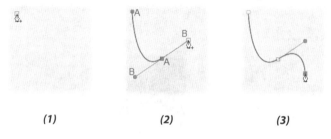

(1)   *(2)*   *(3)*

A = on-curve node
B = off curve control handle

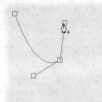

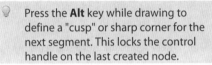
Press the **Alt** key while drawing to define a "cusp" or sharp corner for the next segment. This locks the control handle on the last created node.

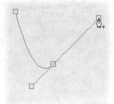

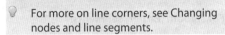
Press the **Ctrl** key while drawing to adjust the active "off-curve" control handle length independently of its partner control handle (belonging to a separate segment).

For more on line corners, see Changing nodes and line segments.

Drawing shapes

When a line (or series of line segments) forms a complete, enclosed outline, it becomes a new **closed** object called a **shape**. Because shapes have an interior region that can be filled (for example, with a solid colour or a bitmap), they have fill properties as well as line properties.

You can make a shape by closing a curve—extending a freeform line or a segmented straight line back to its starting point. Shapes have an interior which is filled with the current **default fill** (see Setting fill properties on p. 147) when the shape is closed.

To close an existing curve (with a straight line):

1. Select the curve with the **Node Tool**, **Pencil** or **Pen Tool**.

2. Click ⟍ **Close Curve** on the context toolbar. A Straight segment appears, closing the curve.

To close a curve (without new segment):

- Select the curve with the **Node Tool**, and drag from an end node (note the ▷ Node cursor), moving the line, onto the other end node (a Close cursor will show); releasing the mouse button will create a shape.

If you're trying to draw a cartoon outline made up of many independent curves (e.g., a cartoon ear, rose) and you want to retain the fill colour, you can fill each curve without closing them. This is made easy by using the **Fill-on-Create** feature.

To fill an unclosed curve automatically:

- Select the Pencil Tool, Pen Tool, or Paintbrush Tool.

- Enable ⟨⟩ **Fill-on-Create** from the context toolbar, and select a suitable fill from the Colour tab. You'll also need to ensure **Select-on-Create** is enabled on the context toolbar (Freehand and Paintbrush tools only).

- Draw a freeform line, pen line, or brush stroke into a curve. The resulting curve is closed automatically and filled with the current fill colour.

Editing lines and shapes

To edit lines or shapes, you can manipulate their segments, on-curve nodes, and off-curve control handles allowing you to:

- Redraw part of a line

- Reshape a line

- Simplify a line (remove nodes)

- Enhance a line (add nodes)

- Change the type of node or line segment

- Convert to straight line segments

- Adjust a shape

- Join two lines together

> The procedures below relate to lines drawn with the Pencil Tool, but also to curves drawn with the Pen Tool. For simplicity, we'll only use the term 'line'.

Redrawing part of a line

With the **Pencil Tool**, it's easy to redraw any portion of a line.

To redraw part of a selected line:

1. Select the line, then the ✏ **Pencil Tool**. Hover the displayed cursor on the line where you want to begin redrawing. The cursor changes to indicate you can begin drawing.

2. Click on the line, and a new node appears.

3. Keep the mouse button down and drag to draw a new line section, connecting it back to another point on the original line. Again, the cursor changes to include a curve when you're close enough to the line to make a connection. When you release the mouse button, the original portion is replaced by the newly drawn portion.

Reshaping a line

The main tool for editing lines and shapes is the **Node Tool**. In general, you first use the **Node Tool** to select one or more nodes on the object, then use the buttons on the tool's supporting context toolbar.

To reshape a curved line:

1. Click the ⬦ **Node Tool** on the **Drawing** toolbar.

2. Select any line on your page. The line's on-curve nodes appear, and the context toolbar also pops up.

3. Hover over a segment and drag the segment to form a new curve shape.

-or-

Select nodes and drag. Selection can be by one of the following methods:

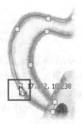 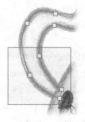 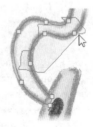

*Hover over a single node and click to select the node. **Shift**-click for multiple nodes.*

Drag out a marquee to select multiple neighbouring nodes

*Drag out a lasso (with **Alt** key pressed) to select multiple nodes otherwise difficult to select via a marquee.*

 Once a square **end node** or **interior node** is selected, the node becomes highlighted and off-curve rounded **control handles** for all line segment(s) will appear. A single control handle shows on an end node; a pair of handles will show on a selected interior node.

Remember that a segment is the line between two nodes; each node provides two control handles, with each handle controlling different adjoining segments. One control handle in a segment works in conjunction with the control handle on the opposite end of the segment.

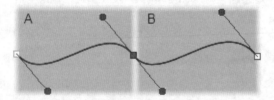

(A) Line Segment 1, (B) Line Segment 2

🖎 For clarity, control handles that do not influence the shape of the line are not displayed. However, each selected node reveals both control handles for manipulation.

4. Drag any selected node to reshape adjacent segment(s). All selected nodes move in the same direction, so you can reshape the curve in complex ways by selecting specific nodes. **Shift**-drag to constrain the movement to horizontal or vertical.

5. Drag one or more control handles to produce very precise changes in the curvature of the line on either side of a node. You can shorten or lengthen the handles, which changes the depth of the **curve** (that is, how far out the curve extends), or alter the handle angle, which changes the curve's **slope**.

🖎 When using the Pen Tool, pressing the **Ctrl** key while clicking a node lets you edit the curve directly. This saves having to jump back to the Node Tool. You can't edit multiple nodes simultaneously.

🖎 By changing the type of node you can change how the adjacent segments behave.

🖎 As a shortcut when selecting nodes, you can press **Tab** or **Shift-Tab** to select the next or previous node along the line (following the order in which nodes were created).

Simplifying or enhancing a line

The more nodes there are on a line or shape, the more control over its shape you have. The fewer nodes there are, the simpler (smoother) the line or shape. You can adjust the **Smoothness** to refine the curve most recently drawn (as long as the line is still selected). It is also possible to add or delete nodes to simplify or enhance curves, and even clean curves (removing unnecessary nodes automatically).

To adjust the smoothness of the most recent pencil line:

1. Choose the 🖉 **Pencil Tool** and draw a freeform line.

2.   From the context toolbar, click the right arrow on the **Smoothness** option and drag the displayed slider left to increase the number of nodes (you can also add absolute values into the input box).

3.   To make the curve less complex, i.e., smoother, drag the slider right to decrease the number of nodes.

To add or delete a node:

•   To **add a node**, click along a line segment with the Node Tool or Pen Tool to add a new node at that point. The new node will be created and will be selected (complete with attractor nodes as necessary).

•   ▱ To **delete a node**, select the line with the Node Tool then the node itself and click the **Delete Node** button on the context toolbar (or press the **Delete** key). The node will be deleted, along with any associated attractor nodes, and the line or shape will jump to its new shape. With the Pen Tool selected, you can also delete a node by clicking on it.

You can also use the Node Tool to reposition the nodes, and reshape the line or shape, by dragging on the new handles.

Changing nodes and line segments

Each segment in a line has a control handle at either end, so at each interior or "corner" node (where two segments join) you'll see a pair of handles. The behaviour of these handles—and thus the curvature of the segments to either side—depends on whether the node is set to be **sharp**, **smooth**, **symmetric**, or **smart**. You can quickly identify a node's type by selecting it and seeing which button is selected in the displayed context toolbar. Each type's control handles behave differently as illustrated below.

To change one or more nodes to a different type:

1.   Select the object with the **Node Tool**, followed by the node(s) you want to change.

2. Click one of the node buttons (described below) on the displayed context toolbar.

   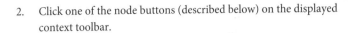 A **Sharp Corner** means that the line segments to either side of the node are completely independent so that the corner can be quite pointed.

   A **Smooth Corner** uses Bézier curves, which means that the slope of the line is the same on both sides of the node, but the depth of the two joined segments can be different.

   At a **Symmetric Corner**, nodes join line segments with the same slope and depth on both sides of the node.

   Smart Corner nodes automatically determine slope and depth for a rounded, best-fitting curve. If you attempt to adjust a smart corner's handles, it becomes a smooth corner. You can always reset the node to smart—but to maintain smart nodes, be careful what you click on!

   Note: Normally, custom segments you draw with the Pen Tool end in a smart corner.

You can also use the context toolbar to define a line segment as either straight or curved.

To change a line segment from straight to curved, or vice versa:

1. With the **Node Tool**, select the leading node of the line segment (the node nearer the start of the line).

2. Then, either:

   - To make a line segment straight, click **Straighten Line** on the context toolbar. The selected segment immediately jumps to a straight line.

     - or -

- To make a line segment curved, click one of the node buttons on the context toolbar: **Sharp Corner**, **Smooth Corner**, **Symmetric Corner**, or **Smart Corner**. You can then adjust the curvature of the newly created curved segment.

To convert to straight lines:

1.   With the Node Tool, select the curve.

2.   From the context toolbar, choose ⋀ **Convert to Straight Lines**. The curve segments are replaced by straight line segments throughout the line.

Adjusting a shape

As described on p. 67, you can easily turn a curve into a shape by connecting its end nodes. You can go the other way, too—break open a shape in order to add one or more line segments.

To break open a line or shape:

1.   With the **Node Tool**, select the node on the closed curve where you want the break to occur.

2.   Click ⁞→⁞ **Break Curve** on the context toolbar so that the line will separate. A shape will become a line with the selected node split into two nodes, one at each end of the new line.

3.   You can now use the Node Tool to reposition the nodes and reshape the line by dragging on the handles.

Joining lines together

You can connect any two straight or curved lines to form a new line.

To join two lines together:

1.   Select both lines by **Shift**-clicking with any selection tool.

2.   Choose **Join Curves** from the **Tools** menu. The end control node of one line is connected with the start control node of the other.

Using QuickShapes

QuickShapes are pre-designed objects that you can instantly add to your page, then adjust and morph into a variety of further QuickShapes. QuickShapes are added from a flyout containing a wide variety of commonly used shapes, including boxes, arrows, hearts, spirals and other useful symbols.

Morphing to new shapes can be carried out as you add the QuickShape to the page via the **QuickShape Creator** dialog or anytime after adding to the page.

To create a QuickShape:

1. Click the down arrow on the ▢▾ **QuickShape** button on the **Drawing** toolbar, then select a shape from the flyout. The button takes on the icon of the shape you selected.

2. At your chosen cursor position, either:

    • Click and drag on the page to draw out your QuickShape to a chosen size (use the **Shift** key to lock the aspect ratio; the **Ctrl** key to scale from its centre point; or both together).

    - or -

1. Double-click to launch the QuickShape Creator, to define the QuickShape explicitly.

2. From the dialog, enter a type, dimensions, and QuickShape-specific parameters.

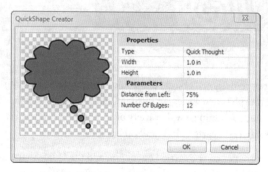

3. Click **OK**.

New QuickShapes adopt the currently set line and fill in DrawPlus.

💡 **Ctrl**-double-click to place a default-sized QuickShape on the page.

All QuickShapes can be positioned, resized, rotated, and filled. What's more, you can "morph" their designs once on the page. For example, dragging the handles on a Quick Polygon will change the number of sides to make a triangle, pentagon, hexagon, or other polygon.

To adjust the appearance of a QuickShape:

1. Click on the QuickShape to reveal sliding handles around the shape. These are distinct from the "inner" selection handles. Different QuickShapes have different handles.

2. Drag any handle to change the appearance of the QuickShape.

For example, by dragging the top sliding handle to the right on the pentagon below will quickly produce an octagon:

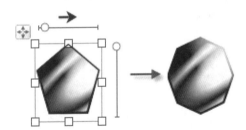

> 💡 You can use the QuickShape context toolbar to swap the QuickShape type for another, as well as the object's line properties; use the Colour or Swatch tab to apply the QuickShape's fill.

Converting a shape to editable curves

The conversion of QuickShapes to curves provides you with a starting point for your own shapes, whereas converting text to curves is one way of incorporating editable letter-based shapes into designs.

To convert an object into curves:

1. Select your QuickShape or text object.

2. Click ⬡ **Convert to Curves** on the Arrange tab.

3. Edit the curve outline using the **Node Tool** (see Editing lines and shapes on p. 68).

However they were created, all converted objects behave in a similar manner. For example, you can create some text with the Artistic Text Tool, convert it to curves, then use the Node Tool to edit the curves that make up the letters, just as if you had drawn the letter shapes by hand using the line tools.

> 🗦 The conversion process loses all of the special properties inherent in QuickShapes and text.

Connectors

Connectors are special lines that you can anchor to objects, where they remain attached even if one or both objects are moved or resized. Using connectors, you can easily create dynamic diagrams and charts that show relationships, such as family trees, organization charts, and flow charts. If you need to rearrange the elements, the connections are preserved.

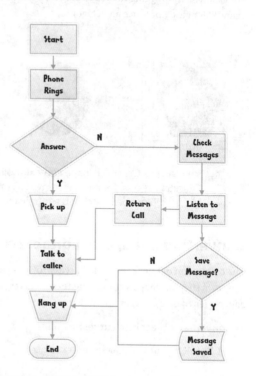

💡 Try the Gallery tab (Office folder) for flow chart (above), network, and organization chart symbols, then simply add connectors between objects.

A key feature of connectors is that if you move any connected object at a later date, the connectors will follow.

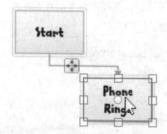

To create a connection:

1. Select 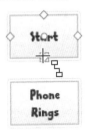 **Connector Tool** on the Line Tools flyout (**Drawing** toolbar). Hover over an object so that default connection points become visible.

    Each DrawPlus object has **default connection points**, displayed whenever you select one of the connector tools and hover over the object. These default points can't be moved or deleted, and are always diamond shaped.

2. On the displayed context toolbar, ensure **Auto Connector Tool** is selected. This creates intelligent Auto Connectors.

3. Click the connection point on the object and drag to the destination object—you'll see potential "target" connection points display (in red) on the destination object. When the pointer is over a chosen connection point release the mouse button. (You'll see a box appear around the point when a connection is imminent.) A connector line will appear between the two connection points.

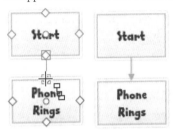

Once you've created a connector, DrawPlus makes it easy to adjust the connector's path or edit the properties of a connector.

To adjust a selected connector's path:

- (For Auto Connectors) Drag the line from the displayed arrows into a new position.

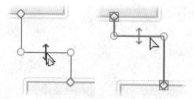

- (For Auto, Right Angle, or Custom connectors) Drag a node(s) to a new position on the page.

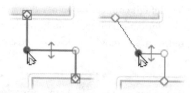

To edit the selected connector's properties (line colour, width, style, and end):

- Select options from the Connector context toolbar at the top of your workspace.

To branch connectors:

- Use **Ctrl+Alt**-drag to copy a connector and connected object simultaneously—great for creating branched connectors. Select the connected object only in advance.

Connector types

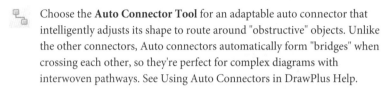 We've used the Auto Connector Tool exclusively so far. However, this tool exists among a selection of connector tools, each designed for different uses. The **Connector Tool**, when selected, offers the different types of connector tool on the Connectors context toolbar situated above the workspace.

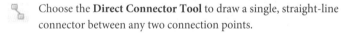 Choose the **Auto Connector Tool** for an adaptable auto connector that intelligently adjusts its shape to route around "obstructive" objects. Unlike the other connectors, Auto connectors automatically form "bridges" when crossing each other, so they're perfect for complex diagrams with interwoven pathways. See Using Auto Connectors in DrawPlus Help.

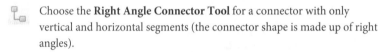 Choose the **Direct Connector Tool** to draw a single, straight-line connector between any two connection points.

Choose the **Right Angle Connector Tool** for a connector with only vertical and horizontal segments (the connector shape is made up of right angles).

To change the connector type:

1. Select the connector with the **Pointer Tool**.

2. Select an Auto, Right Angle, Direct, or Custom connector type from the context toolbar.

- or -

- Right-click the connector and choose equivalent options from the Connectors flyout.

Adding dimension lines and labels

DrawPlus lets you add **dimension lines** with text **labels** showing the distance between two fixed points in a drawing, or the angle formed by three points. For example, you can draw a dimension line along one side of a box, measuring the distance between the two corner points. If you resize the box, the line automatically follows suit, and its label text updates to reflect the new measurement.

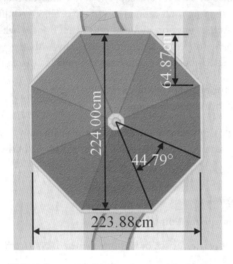

You'll find dimension lines indispensable for planning garden designs (e.g., a garden gazebo plan), technical diagrams, floor plans, or any drawing where exact measurements and scale are important.

Although they can be drawn anywhere on the page, dimension lines are at their most accurate when attached to **connection points** on objects (see p. 78) or when snapped to **dynamic guides** (see p. 44).

- **Connection points**

  When you choose one of the Dimension tools, connection points on page objects become visible on hover over, i.e., when you move the mouse pointer directly over a connection point, a small box appears around it when a connection can be made. The line can then be connected to the object's connection point.

- **Dynamic guides**
  You can snap a dimension line to a dynamic guide, creating "free-floating" dimension lines that don't actually touch objects (see previous page). Use this for neatly presenting horizontal or vertical dimension lines. Guides will be offered to snap to when your line approaches objects on the page.

To draw a dimension:

1. Select the ⯊ **Dimension Tool** from the **Drawing** toolbar's Line Tools flyout. (The flyout shows the icon of the most recently selected tool.)

2. Either, for a **linear dimension**, click the respective tool from the Dimension context toolbar:

   - ⯊ **Auto Dimension Line Tool**
     Use to draw vertical, horizontal, or diagonal dimension lines in any direction, with automatic placement of the editable dimension label adjacent to the line

   - ⯊ **Vertical Dimension Line Tool**
     Ideal for vertical dimension lines, the label information is always presented vertically with the option to move the label by dragging. Extension lines are used to present the dimension line vertically and to allow for an optional offset.

   - ⯊ **Horizontal Dimension Line Tool**
     As above but for horizontal dimension lines.

   - ⯊ **Slanted Dimension Line Tool**
     Designed specifically for drawing diagonal dimension lines.

   Click where you want to start the dimension line (e.g., on a connection point), then drag and release the mouse button where you want to end the line (maybe on another connection point).

The illustrations below show the result of dragging between connection points on two Quick Squares with the **Vertical Dimension Line Tool** enabled.

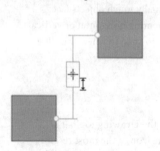
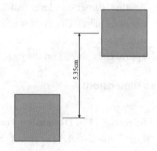

A pair of parallel **extension lines** with end **nodes** appears from the two points. Between the two extension lines, the dimension line and its label "float". Click the blue line box to position the floating line and label; drag the red circle within.

Release when the line and label are where you want them. (You can always change the positions later.) Click away to reveal the dimension line.

- or -

For an **angular dimension**, click the ⬚ **Angular Dimension Line Tool** then click on a point along one side of the desired angle, then drag and release the mouse button at a point along the other side of the angle (points A and B in the illustration). Click again at the vertex of the angle (point C). These three points define the starting and ending sides of the angle. Between the two sides, the angle's arc and its label "float," awaiting final positioning. Click again to position the floating elements.

> Angles are measured anti-clockwise from the starting to the ending side, so choose your three nodes accordingly

To complete the dimension line, move the mouse again to position the floating line or arc and its label—note that they respond independently—and click when they are where you want them. (You can always change the positions later.) The dimension line appears.

Once you've added a dimension line, you can freely adjust node/label positions, format the line, and format the label text via context toolbars.

Using the Gallery

The Studio's Gallery tab contains pre-built design objects and elements you'd like to reuse in different drawings. You can choose designs stored under Clipart, Home, Office, School, ShapeArt, and Web folders.

The Gallery tab has two parts: an upper **Folder/Categories** drop-down menu and a lower **Designs** window where you can select and drag a copy of the design onto your page.

The Gallery tab also lets you store your own designs in a **My Designs** section if you would like to reuse them—the design is made available in any DrawPlus document. You can add and delete your items within each category, with the option of naming elements to facilitate rapid retrieval.

> You can create your own folders and categories from the Gallery
> tab's ▷ **Tab Menu**.

To view your Gallery:

- Click the Studio's **Gallery** tab.

- Select a folder or category from the drop-down menu. The items from the folder's first listed category are displayed by default.

To use a design from the Gallery:

- Drag any preset design directly onto the page. You can modify, then drag the design back into your own custom category.

To copy an object into the Gallery:

1. Display the Gallery tab's **My Designs** (or sub-category of that) where you want to store the object.

2. Drag the object from the page and drop it onto the gallery.

3. You'll be prompted to type a name for the design. (You can name or rename the design later, if you wish.) By default, designs are labelled as "Untitled."

4. A thumbnail of the design appears in the gallery, labelled with its name.

To delete or rename a custom design:

*   Right-click its gallery thumbnail and choose **Delete Design...** or **Rename Design...** from the submenu.

Using graphic styles

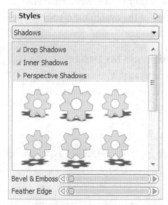

The **Styles tab** contains multiple galleries of pre-designed styles that you can apply to any object, or customize to suit your own taste! Galleries exist in effect categories such as 3D, Bevels, Blurs, Edges, Shadows, and other 2D and 3D filter effects, with each category having further subcategories.

A key feature of graphic styles is that when a style is applied to an object it complements the object's other properties, rather than replaces them. As an example, if an object already had a line colour and fill, these properties would be maintained after adding, e.g., a perspective shadow. However, if another shadow style is applied, it will replace the perspective shadow.

The Styles tab also lets you store your own graphic styles in a **My Styles** section if you would like to reuse them—the style is made available in any DrawPlus document. You can add and delete your items within each category, with the option of naming elements to facilitate rapid retrieval.

 You can create your own folders and categories from the Style tab's ▷ **Tab Menu** by selecting **Manager...** from the menu.

To apply a graphic style to one or more objects:

1. Display the **Styles** tab.

2. Expand the drop-down menu to select a named style category (e.g., Instant Effects), then pick a subcategory by scrolling the lower window.

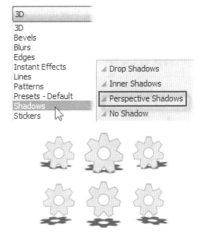

3. Preview available styles as thumbnails (cog shapes are shown by default) in the window.

4. Click a style thumbnail to apply it to the selected object(s).

Saving custom graphic styles

Once you've come up with a set of attributes that you like—properties for fill, line, text, and 2D/3D effects, and so on—you can save this cluster of attributes as a named **graphic style**. DrawPlus saves graphic styles to the Styles tab (My Styles folder by default), which can be subsequently applied to other newly drawn objects.

For example a Quick Star can have a stone effect applied via a previously saved graphic style (a cog shape is used as the default preview type).

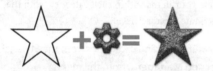

To create a new graphic style based on an existing object's attributes:

1. Select **Create Graphic Styles...** from the **Format** menu.

The Graphic Style Editor dialog appears, with a list of graphic properties and attributes on the left and a four-pane preview region, showing how the graphic style looks on sample objects (Cog, Rounded Rectangle, Sample Text, or the Letter A).

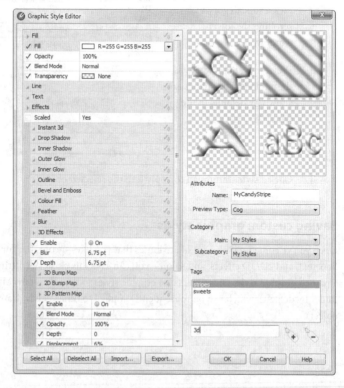

2. (Optional) Click to expand or collapse sections within the list of attributes. This reveals which attributes are currently set. Uncheck any attributes you want to exclude from the style definition, or check any you want to additionally include.

3. (Optional) If you want to modify any attribute, select its value and edit via flyout, drop-down list, dialog, or input box.

4. Type a **Name** to identify the style thumbnail, and optionally, save to a different **Preview Type** (see above) instead of the default cog shape; this preview type will show in the Styles tab.

5. Select the Style tab's **Main** category and **Subcategory** where you want to save the style thumbnail to. Styles are saved to the tab's My Styles category by default. You'll need to create any custom categories in advance.

6. (Optional) To help find styles in the Styles tab, add tags to your style definition by entering text (e.g., 3d) and clicking the **Add Tag** button. You'll be able to search for the style via the Styles tab. See Finding styles on p. 90.

7. Click **OK**. A thumbnail for the new graphic style appears in the designated Styles tab category.

Once a graphic style is listed in a gallery, you can modify it or create a copy (for example, to define a derivative style) by right-clicking on its thumbnail and choosing **Edit Style...** or **Copy Style...**.

To create a graphic style from scratch:

1. In the Styles tab, navigate to a category in which you want to create your new style.

2. Click ✚ **Add New Graphic Style**.

3. From the dialog, configure attributes via flyout, drop-down list, dialog, or input box.

Importing and exporting graphic styles

DrawPlus can import individual graphic styles created by colleagues and friends who also use DrawPlus X5. The reverse is true also—if you've created an exciting new graphic style you can share it just as easily. Styles are saved in a Graphic Style File (.gstyle). Use **Import...** and **Export...** in the Graphic Style Editor dialog for importing and exporting.

Finding graphic styles

The Styles tab offers a Find Style feature which lets you locate preset or custom graphic styles saved previously. Partial matching is supported, e.g. a search for "shadow" will find styles named "MyShadow", "Outer Shadow 2", "Lift Shadow 1".

To find a graphic style:

1. From the Styles tab's ▷ **Tab Menu**, select **Find Style...**.

2. In the dialog, Enter a style name to search for.

3. Click **OK**. The search results are displayed in a temporary Search Finished folder.

A found style can be applied to a selected object as for any other graphic style in the Styles tab.

5 Using Brushes

Selecting brushes

DrawPlus supports a wide range of brushes, all capable of producing:

Stroke brush effects:

- Draw (graphic pencil, marker pen, pen, pencil)

- Paint (bristle, stipple, wash)

Spray and photo brush effects:

- Airbrush, splats, spray can

- Effects (bubbles, glitter, neon, smoke, fur, clouds)

- Grunge

- Nature (fog, grass, snow)

- Photo (rope, chains, zippers, flowers, embroidery, textured edges)

Painting inherits the principles of Drawing lines and shapes (see p. 61). The drawing freedom of the Pencil Tool is adapted for brushwork using the dedicated Paintbrush Tool. You can pick up colour for your brushes as you would for other object, by simply selecting the Paintbrush Tool, choosing your **brush type** from the **Brushes tab** and picking a brush colour from context toolbar, Colour or Swatch tab.

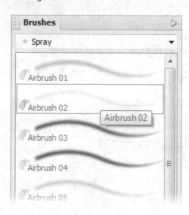

The Brushes tab lets you **select** a brush type from a range of categories. You can also view brushes currently being used in your document, and edit brushes (p. 96) or create your own brushes (see DrawPlus Help).

Stroke and spray brush types are indicated by symbols.

To make sense of all the brush types available to the user, the preset brushes are stored under a series of pre-defined categories under the name **Global**—the brushes are available to all DrawPlus documents currently open. The **Document** category shows the brush types currently in use in the DrawPlus drawing and is used to "bookmark" brushes for easy reuse in the future.

At some point, you may want to edit, copy or create your own stroke or spray brush type. See DrawPlus Help.

Brush strokes can be applied directly to the page by using your mouse or pen tablet; the latter method is ideally suited for applying pressure-sensitive strokes to your drawing. However, painting with the mouse still provides a viable alternative to the tablet, where pressure sensitivity is controlled via the Pressure tab or set on a per brush basis.

Applying brush strokes

The **Paintbrush Tool** is used exclusively to apply brush strokes to the page. The tool is used in conjunction with the Brushes tab, and a supporting context toolbar.

To apply a brush stroke:

1. Select the **Paintbrush Tool** from the **Drawing** toolbar.

2. Display the Brushes tab and choose a category from the drop-down list, then a brush.

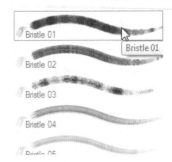

3. Select a **Line Colour**, **Width**, or **Opacity** from the Brush context toolbar.

4. (Optional) For spray brushes, adjust **Flow** to control the density of paint laid down as you apply it, like "layering up" a brush then painting.

5. (Optional) From the context toolbar, adjust **Smoothness** (to set how smooth your stroke is applied).

6. (Optional) Enable **Select-on-Create** to leave the brush stroke selected on the page. If disabled, the stroke is left deselected.

7. (Optional) Enable **Fill-on-Create** to fill the unclosed curve produced by the brush stroke with the default fill colour.

8. With the brush cursor, drag across your page to create a brush stroke.

You can also apply a brush stroke around an object's outline (shape, artistic text, picture, etc.) via **Brush Stroke** on the Line tab. See Setting line properties on p. 152.

After this first brush stroke, there are two ways in which you are likely to paint subsequently, depending on the extent to which you plan to edit brush strokes as you go. To assist you, the **Select-on-Create** button on the Brushes context toolbar can be used:

- **Edit then Paint**. With the button disabled, the brush stroke is laid down and is immediately deselected. The stroke needs to be reselected to perform any editing. Use when you're happy to set all the brush properties (colour, brush type, width, etc) before painting (as above), especially if you intend to paint repeatedly with the same brush stroke.

- **Paint and Edit**. With the button enabled, a painted brush stroke will remain selected, meaning that the brush stroke can be fine-tuned via the context toolbar immediately. Use when changing your brush properties frequently, e.g. when adjusting a brush stroke's colour, width, opacity or shape. The **ESC** key deselects the current brush stroke.

Setting Brush Defaults

See Updating defaults on p. 30.

Editing brush strokes

It's possible to alter any previously drawn brush stroke with respect to its properties, brush type, and shape.

To change brush stroke properties:

- Use the Brushes context toolbar to adjust the properties of a brush stroke once applied to your page.

To change brush stroke type:

1. Select the brush stroke.

2. Go to the Brushes tab and select firstly a brush category, then a brush type from the displayed gallery. The brush stroke adopts the newly chosen brush. To change the shape of your brush stroke:

A brush stroke possesses very similar characteristics to a plain line. Any brush stroke can therefore be edited, extended, or redrawn with the **Node Tool** (**Drawing** toolbar) just as for a straight or curved line (see Editing lines and shapes on p. 68). Use for fine-tuning your brush strokes after application.

6 Working with Text

Entering text

You can create different types of text in DrawPlus, i.e., **Artistic Text**, **Frame Text**, or **Shape Text**, all directly on the page.

Morbi nisl eros, dignissim nec, malesuada et, convallis quis, augue. Vestibulum ante ipsum primis in faucibus orci luctus et ultrices posuere cubilia Curae; Proin

Artistic Text   **Frame Text**   **Shape Text**

It's easy to edit the text once it's created, by retyping it or altering properties like font, style, and point size.

In general, artistic text (as an independent object) is better suited to decorative or fancy typographic design, frame text is intended for presenting text passages in more traditional square or rectangular shaped blocks; shape text lends itself so well to blocks of body text where shape and flow contribute to the overall layout.

Artistic text behaves more independently than Shape and Frame Text and its individual letters can be stretched, rotated, sheared, enveloped, and combined with other objects. Shape text lacks a line property, but it conforms to the containing shape, and you can achieve unique text flow effects by varying the container's properties. (For more details, see Fitting text to frames and shapes on p. 108.)

Default settings (p. 30) are stored separately for artistic text and frame text.

To enter new artistic text:

1. Select **A** **Artistic Text Tool** on the **Drawing** toolbar's **A·** Text flyout.

2. To create **artistic text** at the current default point size, click where you want to start the text.

    - or -

For artistic text that will be automatically sized into an area, click and drag out the area to the desired size.

3. To set text attributes (font, size, etc.) before you start typing, make selections on the Text context toolbar. For colour, set the Line/Fill swatches on the Studio's Colour or Swatch tab.

4. Start typing.

To create frame text:

1. Select **Frame Text Tool** on the **Drawing** toolbar's Text flyout.

2. From the positioned cursor, either:

   • Double-click on the page to create a new frame at a default size.
   - or -

   • Drag out a frame to your desired frame dimension.

3. (Optional) Set text and colour attributes as for artistic text before you start typing.

4. Start typing within the frame.

To enter new shape text:

1. Create a QuickShape either from the **Drawing** toolbar's QuickShape flyout or by closing a drawn line.

2. With a shape still selected, select **Artistic Text** (**Drawing** toolbar) and just start typing.

For existing shapes without shape text, select the shape, then the **Artistic Text** tool, then begin typing.

Working with Unicode text

On occasion, you may wish to import text in a foreign language, e.g. you may want to include a foreign quote in its original language. To work outside the standard ASCII character set, DrawPlus allows Unicode characters to be pasted (using **Edit>Paste Special...**) from the clipboard into your drawing.

To retain formatting, use "*Formatted Text (RTF)*" or for plain text use "*Unformatted Unicode Text.*"

Editing text

Once you've entered either **artistic**, **frame** or **shape text** (see Entering text on p. 99), you can retype it and/or format its character attributes (i.e., font, point size, bold/italic/underline, subscript/superscript, OpenType font features), paragraph properties, and text flow. Text objects have graphic properties, too: artistic text behaves like an independent graphic object (it can be scaled), while shape or frame text conforms to its container or frame.

Artistic text, text frames, and shapes containing text can all be rotated, skewed, moved, and copied. You can also apply line and fill colour independently, brush strokes/edges, or apply opacity and transparency effects, for interesting text effects.

Colour can be applied to selected text as a solid, gradient or bitmap fill—for a solid fill, simply select one or more characters and apply a solid colour from the Studio's Colour tab (ensuring the fill swatch is set) or the Character dialog. See Setting fill properties on p. 147.

For a gradient or bitmap fill, use the Studio's Swatch tab. See p. 159 or p. 162, respectively.

Similarly, opacity is applied from the Colour tab (see p. 167); gradient and bitmap transparency from the Transparency tab.

Retyping text

You can either retype artistic, frame or shape text directly on the page, or use the Edit Text window—great for managing large amounts of text (overflowed shape text or otherwise) in a simple word processing environment.

To retype text on the page:

1. **A A -** Select the object and then select **Artistic Text** (from the **Drawing** toolbar's Text flyout) in either order.

2. Type new text at the selection point or drag to select text, then type to replace it. To cut, copy, and paste, use the toolbar buttons or standard Windows keyboard shortcuts.

To create a new line:

- At the position you want to start a new line, press the **Enter** key.

Formatting text

You can change text formatting (character, paragraph, bullets/numbering and text flow properties) directly on the page via the Text context toolbar or via a **Text Style** dialog.

In addition, artistic text characters have line properties, expanding their creative possibilities.

To format selected text on the page:

1. **↖ A** Use the **Pointer Tool** to select the text you want to change. Alternatively, drag select on any text with **Artistic Text** (from the **Drawing** toolbar's Text flyout).

2. Use the Text context toolbar to change text properties (font, point size, bold/italic/underline, subscript/superscript, OpenType font features, text alignment, bullets and numbering, levels, and text fitting).
   - or -
   Choose **Character...**, **Paragraph...**, **Tabs...**, **Bullets and Numbering...**, or **Text Flow...** from the **Format** menu (or the right-click menu via **Text>**).

🔖 The ▷ **Node Tool** can be used for special adjustments on artistic text.

🔖 For greater control over the shape of the artistic text characters, try converting the artistic text to **curves**. As curves, you can position every character individually and even edit the character shapes, exactly as if you had drawn the character shapes by hand using the line tools. For details, see Converting a shape to editable curves on p. 77.

Using fonts

If you plan to use text in your drawing, you can change the text's appearance dramatically by changing its font. In doing so you can communicate very different messages to your target audience.

Font assignment is very simple in DrawPlus, and can be done from the Text context toolbar, or in the **Text Style** dialog (via right-click **Text>Character...**, or from **Character...** on the **Format** menu).

A font belongs to one of the following types as indicated by the symbol before the font's name.

𝕋	TrueType	*O*	OpenType
A	Type 1 (PostScript)	🖳	Raster (bitmap)

🔖 As you hover over a font in the drop-down list, you'll get an "on-the-page" live preview of that font on any currently selected artistic or frame text.

Fonts with OpenType features

Microsoft Windows supplies OpenType and TrueType font types as standard.

To extend the capability of your installed OpenType font, DrawPlus allows you to take advantage of additional **font features** built into your font's design. These allow font characters to be changed either via substitution rules or by manual choice. As an example you may see extra **glyphs**, i.e., letter shape variations, appear on the character.

Note that some fonts don't support additional font features, with others supporting only a limited font features. This is dependent on how the font designer has created the font originally. As an example, Windows Vista fonts such as **Constantia**, **Calibri**, and **Cambria** possess limited OpenType font features; the Windows 7 font **Gabriola** has richer features, including selectable stylistic sets. However, if you're involved in advanced typography, it's likely that you've already purchased and installed professional fonts supporting OpenType features.

Font-dependent features may include:

- **Ligatures**
  Replace a pair or triplet of characters such as "fi" of "ffi" with a single glyph. In this case it avoids the problem of the dot of the "i" conflicting visually with the hook of the "f". Discretionary ligatures are not used as standard because they are typically too ornate for standard text, these are more decorative in nature and, as the name implies, are intended to be substituted manually.

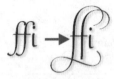

- **Stylistic Sets/Stylistic Alternates**
  Stylistic sets can give you many options of what you want the font to look like and combine preset choices such as which ligatures and alternates are available by default. These can be especially ornate or flowing versions of a glyph (sometimes called "swash" variants). This may be as simple as offering a "g" with and without a closed loop.

$Abc \rightarrow Abc$

- **Small Caps/Petite Caps**
  A small cap "A" should use a special glyph, which typically looks like a capital "A", but is shorter, but has the same stem widths etc. as the capital, so it can't be achieved by just scaling the capital. Petite caps are like small caps but even smaller.

$(CAPS) \rightarrow (CAPS)$

- **Case sensitive forms**
  These are variants of punctuation such as brackets that, for example, are designed to align more nicely with capitals. These would generally sit a little higher in the line, because most capitals don't have descenders.

$12^{th} \rightarrow 12^{th}$

- **Superscripts and subscripts**
  These are smaller raised or lowered versions of characters; the scaling issues are the same as for Small Caps. Some fonts also provide **Ordinals**, which are a form of superscript intended to be used for the letters in "2nd", or forms that are intended to be used in chemical or mathematical notation.

$1/3 \rightarrow \frac{1}{3}$

- **Fractions**
  In text like "1/3", the digits before the slash are made smaller and raised, and the digits after the slash are made smaller and may be lowered. A special narrow version of the slash may be used.

$G12g \rightarrow G12g$

- **Old style figures**
  These are digits that have a bit more character (at right); they often sit lower in the line. Compare with the more usual "lining" figures that are more uniform (at left).

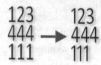

- **Proportional figures**

  These are variable width digits (at right); for example, a "1" that is narrower than a "2", which would look good when set in body text, as opposed to the more usual tabular figures (at left) that are all the same width so they line up in columns or tables.

> ✎ Options vary according to font. If no options are offered, the font does not provide any additional font features.

To apply OpenType features to selected characters:

1. Select your text which has the OpenType font assigned to it.

2. **O ▾** From the Text context toolbar, click the down arrow on the **OpenType flyout**. On the flyout, the displayed options (showing sample text and hover preview) vary according to the features supported by the OpenType font.

	Swashes
sw	BRIGHT VIXENS JUMP; DOZY FOWL QUACK
	Stylistic Sets
ss	Bright vixens jump; dozy fowl quack.
ss2	Bright vixens jump; dozy fowl quack.
ss3	Bright vixens jump; dozy fowl quack.
ss4	BRIGHT VIXENS JUMP; DOZY FOWL QUACK
ss5	BRIGHT VIXENS JUMP; DOZY FOWL QUACK
ss6	BRIGHT VIXENS JUMP; DOZY FOWL QUACK
ss7	BRIGHT VIXENS JUMP; DOZY FOWL QUACK
ss8	BRIGHT VIXENS JUMP; DOZY FOWL QUACK
	Stylistic Alternates
SA	ij Aı Aı Aı Aı Aı Aı Aı Aı Aı
	Miscellaneous OpenType
(A)	Case Sensitive Forms
23	Lining Figures

3. Select an option(s) from the flyout.

To apply OpenType features to text styles:

1. From **Format>Character**, select the **Character - OpenType** option. Expand the tree for all OpenType features.

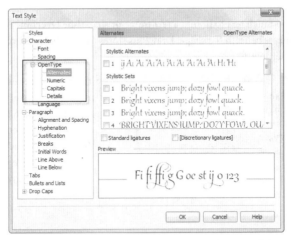

2. Enable font features under the Alternates, Numeric, Capitals, and Details sections.

   - **Alternates**: The OpenType Alternates dialog (above) offers glyph substitutions or alternate representations such as swashes, stylistic sets, contextual alternates, stylistic alternates, and titling alternates.

   - **Numeric**: Offers OpenType features used primarily when setting numbers, e.g. Figure Styles, Figure Width, and Number Position.

   - **Capitals**: Groups case-base features together such as small caps, petite caps, and case-sensitive forms.

   - **Details**: Dynamically displays every OpenType feature in list form, derived from the font's internal tables. As such you can set less common OpenType Features, unavailable from the previous Alternates, Numeric, and Capitals sections.

If an option is shown in brackets it is not supported by the currently used font.

Fitting text to frames and shapes

Text overflow

If there's too much text to fit into a text frame or shape, the **Overflow** button appears beneath the shape; DrawPlus stores the overflowing text in an invisible overflow area.

To make all the text fit you might edit the story down to allow text to fit in the frame or shape. However, scaling the frame or shape text to fit may be preferable so it fits exactly into the available frame.

To scale the frame or shape text:

- Click Overflow to **autofit** the frame or shape text to its container.

  - or -

- Use **Autofit** on the Text context toolbar.

For incremental scaling, use the **Enlarge Text** or **Shrink Text** buttons on the same toolbar.

Positioning

- **Vertical alignment** (right-click **Text>Text Flow...**) moves existing text to the Top, Bottom, or Centre of the container (alternatively you can justify text vertically). The setting anchors a particular part of the object—for example, a "Top" setting anchors the top line and forces new text to come in below, while a "Bottom" setting anchors the bottom (most recent) line and pushes previous lines up as you type new lines.

- To add white space around your text, you can indent text from the frame or shape edge via right-click **Text>Text Flow...**. Values can be set to indent from Left, Right, Top and/or Bottom.

Resizing

- You can resize frame or shape text (change its point size) automatically when resizing frame and shapes. First make sure the **Scale text with item** box is checked in the Text flow dialog (right-click **Text>Text Flow...**) then drag a corner of the selected text object.

Fitting text to a path

DrawPlus allows you to make artistic text conform to a curved baseline (such as a drawn freeform line or curve), custom shape or a preset shape (QuickShape).

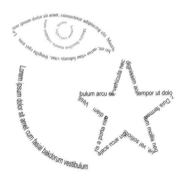

To fit text to a path:

1. Select the curve or shape.

2. Select **A** **Artistic Text** on the **Drawing** toolbar's Text flyout.

3. Hover over the curve or shape's outline until you see a ⌐∿ cursor, then click at the point on the line where your text is to begin.

4. Begin typing your text. The text will be placed along the curve or shape.

To flow text along a preset path:

1. Select your artistic text.

2. From the context toolbar, click the down arrow on the ✕ ▾ **Preset Text Paths** button and select a preset curve from the drop-down menu on which the text will flow.

> ★ You can edit the baseline curve with the Node Tool.

Spell-checking

The **Spell Checker** lets you check the spelling of selected artistic, frame, or shape text, as well as all text sequentially throughout your DrawPlus document.

Multilingual spell checking is supported by use of over 10 spelling dictionaries. By default, the spelling dictionary is set on program install (according to Windows Control Panel's Regional and Language Options), i.e., your dictionary is set to the operating system's language.

Any detected spelling mistakes or any word not present in the language's dictionary will appear underlined with a red zigzag line.

between the pair. The
clock struck midnight..
the man was gone,
forver into the mist-
clad night.

Alternatively, you can use the **Spell Checker** to check through your document, checking for mistakes/unknown words page-by-page.

To enhance the power of spell checking, you can add words to the current dictionary that spell checking doesn't yet know about. These could include uncommon words, technical words, or even acronyms and abbreviations.

To check spelling:

1. (Optional) To check specific text, select the artistic, frame or shape text in advance.

2. Choose **Check Spelling...** from the **Tools** menu.

3. (Optional) In the dialog, click **Options...** to set preferences for ignoring words in certain categories, such as words containing numbers or upper/mixed case characters.

4. Enable **Check currently selected objects only** or **Check all text** radio buttons depending on if you want to spell check text selected previously or all text.

5. Click **Start** to begin the spelling check.

When a problem is found, DrawPlus highlights the problem word on the page. The dialog offers alternative suggestions, and you can choose to **Change** or **Ignore** this instance (or all instances with **Change All** or **Ignore All**) of the problem word, with the option of using **Add** to add the problem word to your dictionary. DrawPlus will also let you **Suggest** an alternative.

6. Spell checking continues until you click the **Close** button or the spell-check is completed.

To change to a different spelling language:

1. Go to **Options...** from the **Tools** menu, and select **Text>Spell Checker**.

2. Choose a different **Language** from the drop-down list, and click **OK**.

> Spell checking can be turned off by selecting "None" as a language type—this could be useful when working with text containing an unmanageable number of unusual terms (perhaps scientific or proprietary terminology).

Using Auto-Correct and Spell as you Type

DrawPlus includes two powerful support tools to nip possible spelling errors in the bud. The **Auto-Correct** feature overcomes common typing errors and lets you build a custom list of letter combinations and substitutions to be applied automatically as you type. You can also **underline mistakes as you type** to mark possible problem words in your text with red underline. Both features apply to frame text, artistic text, or shape text.

If you prefer to address spelling issues in larger doses at the same time, you can run the Spell Checker anytime.

Auto-Correct

To set options for automatic text correction:

1. Choose **Options...** from the **Tools** menu and select the **Text>Auto-Correct>Options** page.

2. Check your desired Auto-Correct options as required.

For any checked options, auto-correction will be enabled. Additionally, a predefined correction list for automatic text replacement can be used; the list, populated by commonly typed misspellings and their correct equivalents, can also be added to for custom corrections.

To use a correction list:

1. Choose **Options...** from the **Tools** menu and select the **Text>Auto-Correct>Replacements** page.

2. Check **Replace text while typing** to turn on Auto-Correct. The predefined text replacements will be applied when you type the misspelt words.

✓ Replace text while typing

Replace: With:

dfwsvssvcsd

1/2	½
1/4	¼
3/4	¾
abotu	about
abouta	about a
aboutit	about it
abscence	absence
accesories	accessories
accidant	accident

To add custom misspellings to the correction list:

1.   In the **Replace** field, type a name for the Auto-Correct entry. This is the abbreviation or word to be replaced automatically as you type. For example, if you frequently mistype "product" as "prodcut," type "prodcut" in the Replace box.

2.   In the **With** field, type the text to be automatically inserted in place of the abbreviation or word in the **Replace** field.

3.   Click the **Add** button to add the new entry to the list.

4.   To modify an entry in the correction list, select it in the list, then edit it in the **Replace** and **With** field above. Click the **Replace** button below.

5.   To remove an entry, select it and click **Delete**.

Spell as you Type

Use this feature to firstly indicate possible problem words in your text using red underline, and secondly to offer (via right-click) a range of alternative correct spellings to replace the problem words.

To check spelling as you type:

- Ensure the **Underline mistakes as you type** feature is turned on (from **Tools>Options>Text>Spell Checker**).

In your document, words with spelling problems are indicated with a red squiggly underline. You can review these by eye, with the option of replacing the words with suggested alternatives.

- To replace a marked word, place an insertion point in a marked word then right-click to choose an alternative spelling from the context menu.

- To tell DrawPlus to ignore (leave unmarked) all instances of the marked word in the drawing, choose **Ignore All** (or just **Ignore** for this instance only).

- To add the marked word (as spelled) to your personal dictionary, choose **Add to Dictionary** from the right-click menu. This means DrawPlus will subsequently ignore the word in any drawing.

- Select **Check Spelling** to run the Spell Checker described above.

> ⚲ You can make your own custom dictionary via **Tools>Options...** (Text>Spelling Dictionary).

7 Working with Objects

Copying, pasting, cutting, and deleting objects

To copy one or more objects to the Windows Clipboard:

1. Select the object(s).

2. Click the **Copy** button on the **Standard** toolbar.

If you're using another Windows application, you can usually copy and paste objects via the Clipboard.

To paste an object from the Clipboard:

- Click the **Paste** button on the **Standard** toolbar.

The standard Paste command inserts a clipboard object onto the page.

> To select the type of object to be pasted from the Clipboard, choose
> **Paste Special...** from the **Edit** menu.

To cut one or more objects to the Clipboard:

1. Select the object(s).

2. Click the **Cut** button on the **Standard** toolbar.

The object is deleted from the page and a copy is placed on the Windows Clipboard.

To delete one or more objects:

- Select the object(s) with the **Pointer**, **Rotate** or **Node Tool** and press the **Delete** key.

Cloning an object

DrawPlus lets you "clone" or duplicate objects easily using drag-and-drop, and duplicate multiple copies of any object. For duplication, a copy is displayed at the new location and the original object is still kept at the same position—your new copy also possesses the formatting of the original copied object.

Making duplicates

- Select the object, then press the **Ctrl** key.

- Drag the object via the  **Move** button to a new location on the page, then release the mouse button.

> Use duplication when rotating or shearing an object—the result is a new copy at a new angle, possibly overlapping the original object.

Making multiple copies in a grid

If you need to clone single or multiple objects, you can use the **Replicate** feature to avoid repetitive copy and paste operations. For example, you can specify three columns and three rows, for nine identical copies (opposite).

To replicate an object:

1. Select an object. Remember to size the object to be cloned and place it in a convenient starting position—usually the top-left of the page.

2. Choose **Replicate...** from the **Tools** menu.

3. In the dialog, set the Grid size by choosing number of columns or rows. Objects are cloned into this grid arrangement (but can be moved subsequently into any position).

4. Set an X and Y spacing (horizontal and vertical gap) between objects if necessary. The feature comes in handy for creating repetitive patterns or producing artwork for label sheets.

5. Click **OK**.

> For replicating multiple objects on different layers, enable the **Edit All Layers** button on the Layers tab. Now, instead of working with the layers one at a time, we can include all objects (once selected) on all layers, permitting perfect replication.

Applying a transform

The Transform feature lets you make multiple copies of one or more selected objects, with a transformation applied to each successive copy in the series.

For example, a butterfly can be made to fly with a transform of 15° rotation, 113% scaling, 4 copies, and an X offset of 1.5cm.

To create a transform:

1. Select an object then choose **Transform...** from the **Tools** menu.

2. From the dialog, specify the type of transformation (rotation and/or scaling), the number of copies, and a positional offset between copies.

✱ Transforms are a quick way to generate elements for a stopframe animation sequence involving rotation or directional changes (see Animation tips and tricks in DrawPlus Help).

Making "in-between" copies of two objects

Blending is yet another useful way of making multiple copies by in-betweening two different objects for a "morphing" effect. For details, see Creating blends on p. 200.

Copying an object's formatting

Format Painter is used to copy one object's line and fill properties directly to another object, including between line/shape and text objects.

To apply one object's formatting to another:

1. Select the object whose formatting you wish to copy.

2. Click ⊤ **Format Painter** on the **Standard** toolbar. When you click the button, the selected object's formatting is "picked up".

3. Click another object to apply the first object's formatting to it. The second object becomes selected.

4. To select another object without pasting the formatting, click it with the **Shift** key down.

5. To cancel Format Painter mode, press **Esc**, click on a blank area, or choose any tool button.

✱ Additional text properties (font, style, and so on) are copied, as well as line and fill properties, when copying formatting from one text object to another.

Moving objects

You can move any selected object anywhere you want and drop it back onto the page or pasteboard by releasing the mouse button.

To move one or more objects:

1. Select the object(s).

2. Click and drag the  **Move** button. The object moves.

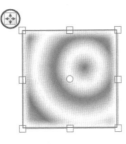

- or -

Click within the selection and drag. Note that the Pointer cursor changes to become a Move cursor.

💡 Use the keyboard arrows to move in increments.

💡 To set exact horizontal and vertical positions, use the Transform tab.

Resizing objects

It's fairly likely that you may want to resize an object to fit into your current design. DrawPlus offers a range of resizing options directly on the object, as well as more precise resizing via keyboard arrows or the Transform tab.

Most objects in DrawPlus maintain their aspect ratio when being resized. One exception is when resizing QuickShapes, as their versatility lend themselves to being resized without constraint.

To resize an object to a fixed aspect ratio:

1. Select the object(s) with the  **Pointer Tool**.

2. Position the cursor over one of the object's handles—you will notice that the cursor changes to a double-headed Size cursor.

3. Drag from a corner handle (above) to resize in two dimensions (by moving two edges), while maintaining the selection's aspect ratio (proportions).

> ➤ To resize to any aspect ratio, with the **Shift** key depressed, drag from an object's corner handle. This resizes in two directions. If you drag an object's side handles, you'll stretch or squash the object in one direction.

> ➤ To resize about the object centre instead, press the **Ctrl** key as you drag.

> 💡 You can also make fine resizing adjustments via the keyboard or from the Transform tab.

To resize QuickShapes:

• As above but the object's aspect ratio is not maintained by default on resize.

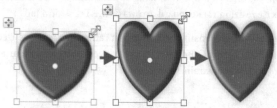

You can use the **Shift** key as you resize to maintain aspect ratio.

Rotating and shearing objects

The **Rotate Tool** lets you both rotate and shear (slant) one or more objects.

To rotate one or more objects around a centre point:

1. Click **Rotate Tool** on the **Drawing** toolbar's Selection flyout.

2. Click to select the object, then hover over a corner handle and, when you see the cursor change, drag in the direction in which you want to rotate the object then release the mouse. (Use **Shift** key for rotating in 15 degree intervals.)

   You'll notice the angle of rotation displayed around the object's centre of rotation ○. Note that when rotating objects, dimensions will be temporarily displayed during the operation.

To change the centre point of rotation:

1. Move the centre of rotation ○ away from its original position to any position on the page. The marker can also be moved to be outside the object—ideal for rotating grouped objects around a central point.

2. Drag the rotate pointer to a new rotation angle—the object will rotate about the new pivot.

Besides being able to rotate an object, the Rotate Tool allows you to skew or "shear" it.

To rotate selected object by set degrees:

- For 90° anti-clockwise: click 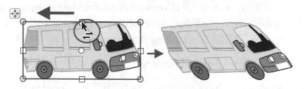 **Rotate 90°** on the **Standard** toolbar.

- For 30°, 45°, 60°, 90°, 180°, 270° anti-clockwise: click the down arrow on the Arrange tab's **Rotate** button and select a value. Once set, clicking the button will rotate the object by the chosen value incrementally.

To shear or copy shear an object:

1. Select **Rotate Tool** on the **Drawing** toolbar's Selection flyout.

2. Click to select the object(s), hover over any side handle (not a corner handle) until you see the Shear cursor.

3. Hold the mouse down and drag the pointer in the direction in which you want to shear the object, then release.

To copy-shear, use the **Ctrl** key while dragging—this preserves the original object, while shearing the new copied object as you drag.

To undo the rotation or shear (restore the original object):

- Double-click the object.

Cutting up objects

It is possible to cut any object (or image for that matter) by using the **Knife Tool** (**Drawing** toolbar). You can cut along a freeform or straight line drawn across your object(s), leaving you with separate fragments of the original.

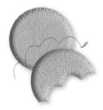 

freeform cut
(using Bump profile)   *straight line cut*

Cutting with a freeform or straight line is possible by drawing the line across the object (or by sweeping the knife cut in and out of the object multiple times in a zig-zag pattern). By hovering over resulting "split" fragments you can click an unwanted fragment to delete. Alternatively, you can deselect the Knife Tool to move the cut fragments apart (see carrot above).

Up to now you may have only performed straight cuts, but you can use the Knife Tool's context toolbar to cut with more sophisticated "shaped" **cutting profiles** (e.g., Wavy, Shark Fin, Bump) or preset knife paths (cookie cutters) based on QuickShapes. The context toolbar is also used to modify any applied cutting profile.

To cut selected objects (freeform or straight line):

> Ensure **Edit All Layers** button on the Layers tab is enabled if you want to cut through selected objects on multiple layers.

1. Select the Knife Tool on the **Drawing** toolbar's Vector Edit flyout.

2. (Optional) Use **Smoothness** on the tool's context toolbar to set how regular the freeform cutting line is—click the right arrow and drag the slider right for increasing smoothness.

3. (Optional) By default, you'll get a straight cutting profile, but for regular-shaped cuts, pick a **Cutting Profile** from the context toolbar.

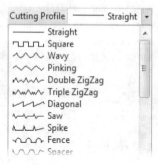

If required, adjust the **Wavelength** and/or **Amplitude** for your shaped cut.

4. Using the cursor, drag a **freeform** line across any object(s) you would like to split (unselected objects on which the line traverses will not be split). Instead, press the **Shift** key as you drag for a **straight** line.

5. Hover over, then click to remove the unwanted cut area(s).

- or -

With the Pointer Tool, drag the newly split fragments apart instead.

Instead of performing a freeform (or straight) cut, you can cut using preset cutter shapes. The cutting shape can be resized or "morphed" to fit your object design, just as for QuickShapes (see p. 75).

To cut out selected objects using cookie cutters:

1. From the Knife Tool's context toolbar, click to expand the **Preset Knife Paths** flyout.

2. Click a preset shape to apply it to your object as a cutout.

The first and second options offer an easy way to jump between freehand and straight line cutting.

3. The shape is applied to the object. Adjust the size and shape using the surrounding square handles and round nodes, respectively.

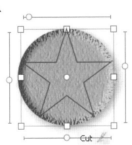

4. Click the **Cut** button in the lower-right corner, then click the unwanted area under the cursor to create your new cutout shape.

Erasing and adding to objects

DrawPlus lets you take a "virtual" eraser to your drawing, letting you remove portions of your selected object(s) on an individual layer or across multiple layers. The extent of erasing can be controlled depending on the tool's currently set erasing nib width and pressure setting (if using a graphics tablet).

The flip side of erasing is "**adding to**" (i.e., augmenting), a technique to add or "grow" a vector object's boundaries—great for reshaping an existing object or to grow a vector shape from scratch. This may be especially useful when creating an unusual filled shape.

To erase portions of a selected object:

1. Select the **Erase Tool** on the **Drawing** toolbar's Vector Edit flyout.

2. (Optional) From the context toolbar, choose a **Nib** style (circle, square, or diamond) and/or set a **Width** to define the erase width that will be cut.

3. Position the cursor, and drag over an object's edge. You'll see the area to be erased area being drawn temporarily (use the **Ctrl** key to redefine the erase area while drawing).

4. Release the mouse button to erase the area drawn.

To add to a selected object:

1. Select the **Freeform Paint Tool** on the **Drawing** toolbar's Vector Edit flyout.

2. (Optional) From the context toolbar, set a **Width** to define the nib width which will be drawn.

3. (Optional) Disable **Select-on-Create** if you want to create new objects every time you use the tool (you might want to create a series of shapes without switching tools).

4. Position the cursor over the object and drag over an object boundary. You'll see shading which represents the area to be added. (You can use the **Ctrl** key to redefine the painted area while holding down the mouse button.)

5. Release the mouse button to reshape the object to include the newly drawn area.

> If you add to or erase from a bitmap, QuickShape, or artistic text, they will be converted to curves, preventing further editing in their original form.

> For Stopframe animation, consider using either tool as a quick way to modify object shapes frame-by-frame.

Cropping and clipping objects

DrawPlus includes some powerful tools for cropping and clipping objects—all hosted on the **Arrange tab**.

Crop and Clip flyout

Provides cropping or clipping functions, where you create a temporary composite object where two or more component objects used to overlap.

This combination, like a group, can be broken apart later with **Crop>Uncrop** on the **Arrange** menu.

• **Crop to Top Object**
 The bottom object is cropped to the outline of the top object.

• **Crop to Bottom Object**
The top object is cropped to the
outline of the bottom object.

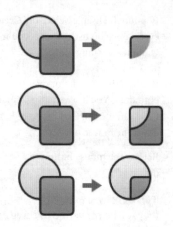

• **Clip to Top Object**
The bottom object is clipped to the
outline of the top object.

• **Clip to Bottom Object**
The top object is clipped to the
outline of the bottom object.

Joining objects

Objects you create on the page can be just the starting point in your design. For
drawn shapes and ready-to-go QuickShapes, it is possible to treat these objects as
"building blocks" in the creation of more complex shapes.

The **Shape Builder Tool** can be used to join together any collection of shapes in
a fun and intuitive way, without the need for prior selection of shapes.

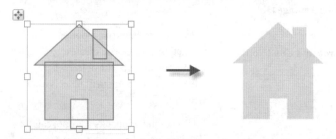

You'll be able to:

- **Add** shapes together by dragging between shapes, making them
  become one (as above).

- **Subtract** intersecting areas with the **Alt** key, a process which would
  otherwise be both difficult and time consuming.

- **Create new shapes**, formed by object overlap, with click and select of
  resulting new object areas.

To add shapes together:

1. Select the  **Shape Builder Tool** on the **Drawing** toolbar.

2. Hover over a shape that overlaps another shape. You'll see a ⬚+ cursor shown on hover over, above a shaded area (to indicate the active region).

3. Drag to the neighbouring shape, using the drawn out dashed line as a guide, then release the mouse button.

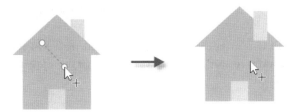

- The properties of the shape lowest in the object order will always be used as the basis for the new shape's properties.

- All shapes under the drawn dashed line will be included in the resulting shape.

As well as adding objects together, DrawPlus lets you take away (or subtract) intersecting areas of overlapping shapes.

To subtract intersecting areas:

1. Select the **Shape Builder Tool** on the **Drawing** toolbar.

2. — Hover over any intersecting area, then **Alt**-click to remove it. You'll see a cursor on hover over.

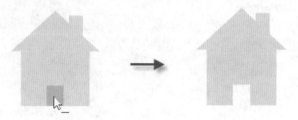

To create new shapes from overlapped shapes:

1. Select the **Shape Builder Tool** on the **Drawing** toolbar.

2. Click once in the chosen area, then select with the **Pointer Tool** (**Drawing** toolbar). You can then drag the new shape to a new position.

Using the Arrange tab

Instead of using the ShapeBuilder Tool, you have the option of using the selection-based Combine tool or "Join" tools such as Add, Subtract, and Intersect.

To combine or join shapes (using Arrange tab):

• Select two objects and choose a tool for the Arrange tab.

Combine

Merges two or more objects into a composite object, with a clear "hole" where their filled regions overlap. The composite takes the line and fill of the bottom object.

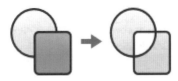

Click the button again to break apart.

Add

Creates one new object that's the sum of any two selected objects, whether or not they overlap.

Add, along with Subtract an Intersect, are Join commands, where you actually produce a permanent new object out of any selected objects. The action can't be reversed, except by using the **Undo** command. A Joined object can be edited with the **Node Tool**, while a combined object cannot.

The objects need not be overlapping.

Subtract

Discards the overlap between the top and bottom object. The top object is also discarded.

Useful as a quick way of truncating shapes and pictures with another object.

Be sure the objects are overlapping!

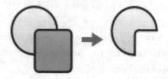

Intersect

Like Subtract, requires overlapping objects—it retains the overlap and discards the rest.

Flipping objects

You can flip selected objects horizontally or vertically.

To flip an object:

- Select the object(s) with one of the selection tools (Pointer, Rotate, or Node).

- To flip the selection left to right, click ⬛ **Flip Horizontal** on the **Standard** toolbar. (Top and bottom stay the same.)

- To flip the selection top to bottom, click  **Flip Vertical** on the same toolbar. (Left and right stay the same.)

> You can use equivalent options on the **Arrange** tab (or **Arrange** menu).

Locking/unlocking an object

To prevent accidentally moving, resizing, flipping, or rotating an object, you can lock it in position.

To lock/unlock an object:

1. Select the single or grouped object.

2. Choose **Lock Position** or **Unlock Position** from the **Arrange** menu. When you lock the object, the cursor changes to a lock symbol.

> You can still alter a locked object's fill, line, or transparency properties.

> In the Layers tab, you can prevent an object from being moved or modified. Simply right-click the object and select **Freeze**.

Grouping objects

Group

The advantage of converting a set of objects into a group is that it is easier to select and edit the objects all at the same time. The only requirement for grouping is that multiple objects are selected in advance (see p. 59).

To create a group from a multiple selection:

- Click **Group** below the selection.

To ungroup (turn a group back into a multiple selection):

- Click **Ungroup** below the selection.

To ungroup multiple groups within a group:

- Select **Ungroup All** from the **Arrange** menu.

Once grouped, simply clicking on any member of a group selects the group object. In general, any operation you carry out on the group affects each member of the group. Property changes applied to a group—such as changing line or fill—will alter all the objects that make up the group.

> 💡 Objects within groups can be selected with **Ctrl**-click and edited without having to ungroup your grouped objects.

> 💡 Groups can have composite opacity applied; this property belongs to the group instead of its group objects.

Aligning and distributing objects

Alignment involves taking a group of selected objects and aligning or distributing them, or both—the operation is applied to all of the objects selected.

To align two or more objects:

1. Using the **Pointer Tool**, **Shift**-click on all the objects you want to align, or draw a marquee box around them (or use **Edit>Select All**), to create a multiple selection.

2. From context toolbar, Align tab, or **Arrange>Align Objects**, select an option for vertical alignment (Align Top, Centre Vertically, or Align Bottom) or horizontal alignment (Align Left, Centre Horizontally,

Align Right) of an object. Object means the last selected object for **Shift**-click multiple selection or the farthest back in Z-order for marquee multiple selection.

To align one or more objects with a page edge:

- Follow the steps above, but check the **Include Page** option.

If selected, the page is added to the set of objects included in the alignment, e.g. selecting **Align Top** aligns all of the objects in the selection to the top of the page. If only one object is selected, page-edge alignment is automatic.

You can distribute objects, so that your objects (as a multiple selection) are spread evenly between the endmost objects on your page. Alternatively, check the **Spaced** option and corresponding measurement value to set a specific distance between each object.

To distribute two or more objects:

1. Using the **Pointer Tool**, **Shift**-click on all the objects you want to distribute, or draw a marquee box around them, to create a multiple selection.

2. In the Align tab, select   **Distribute Horizontally** or **Distribute Vertically** to distribute objects vertically or horizontally, respectively.

3. Check the **Spaced** option to set a fixed distance between vertically or horizontally distributed objects (otherwise the objects distribute evenly between endmost items).

Ordering objects

Think of the objects on a page as being stacked or piled on top of each other. The front-most object is the one on top of the stack. Each time you create a new object, it goes in front of the objects already there. But you can move any object to any **depth** in the ordering sequence, and obtain sophisticated drawing effects by learning how to manipulate the front/back relationship of objects.

As an example, we've used a camera lens to illustrate ordering.

Notice how the lens possesses a "realistic" look by blending overlapped composite objects.

Gradient and solid fills combine to simulate three-dimensional objects (with reflections, highlights and shading).

> ⭐ Don't confuse the concept of object ordering with that of layers in the document. Layers are created by the artist to logically separate sections of a design for better drawing management. Within a layer, objects are ordered with the topmost object being in front of all other objects in that layer; the bottom object, being behind all other layer objects.

To change the selected object's order (dynamically via slider):

- From the Arrange tab, drag the **Depth** slider left to place the object further down the object order (within its layer); drag right to place object further up the order. Ordering occurs as you drag.

To change the selected object's order (via ordering buttons):

- To shift the selected object's position to the front of other objects (on top), choose **Bring to Front** on the **Standard** toolbar (or Arrange tab).

- To shift the selected object's position behind other objects (on the bottom), choose **Send to Back** on the **Standard** toolbar (or Arrange tab).

- 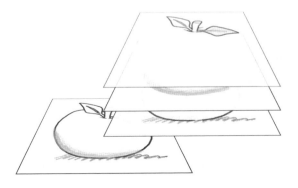 To shift the object's position one step toward the front, choose **Forward One** on the Arrange tab.

- To shift the object's position one step toward the back, choose **Back One** on the Arrange tab.

Working with layers

If you are drawing something simple, you don't really need to make use of layers—you can do all your work on the single layer that every new document has. However, if you're creating something a little more tricky then layers can be a vital aid in separating objects into independent sets. You can think of layers as transparent sheets of paper upon which you can draw your objects.

Layers are useful when you're working on a complex design where it makes sense to separate one cluster of objects from another. The whole drawing is produced by piling up the layers and viewing all of the objects on all of the layers; you can choose which layer you are editing and thus make changes without fear of modifying anything on another layer. In essence, by building up your drawing from multiple layers you make it much easier to edit.

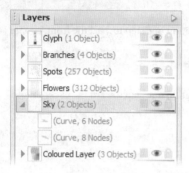

Each layer is situated along with other layers (if present) within a stack on the **Layers tab**—the uppermost layer is applied over any lower layer on the page. You can also expand each layer entry for a tree view of objects associated with that layer (see the Sky layer opposite). Each object entry can be clicked to select the object in your workspace, and you can name your objects at any time.

The tab allows layers to be created, renamed, deleted, reordered, "frozen," and merged.

Thumbnail previews of each layer or object show before each entry—hover your cursor over the thumbnail for a larger preview.

In order to create a new object on a particular layer, you'll first need to "activate" (select) that layer.

To select a particular layer:

- Click a layer name in the Layers tab.

To add a new layer:

- In the Layers tab, click the 🕂 **Add Layer** button to add a new layer above the currently selected layer.

To rename a layer:

- To rename a layer to something more meaningful, click on the selected layer's name and type to add your new name (you can also make an insertion point to edit the existing text). A good example would be to rename the initial Layer 1 to be called Sky (as above).
  - or-

- Double-click the layer and edit the **Name** field in the Layer Properties dialog. See Studio: Layers tab in DrawPlus Help for more details.

To delete a layer:

- In the Layers tab, select the layer's name and click the ⬚ **Delete Layer** button.

> 🔖 If you delete a layer, all of the objects on it are lost! So if you want to keep any of them, move them to another layer first.

You can move layers up or down in the stacking order to place their objects in front or behind those on other layers, move objects to specific layers, and even merge layers.

To move a layer in the stacking order:

- ⬘ ⬙ In the Layers tab, select the layer's entry, then click the **Move Layer Up** or **Move Layer Down** button to move the layer up or down in the list, respectively.

  - or -

- Drag the selected layer to a new position in the layer stack.

Remember that objects on layers are drawn in the order in which the layers were initially added to the Layers tab. Put another way: the bottom layer in the Layers tab stack is drawn first then the second bottom, third bottom etc. A background layer should be the bottom layer in the Layers tab stack.

The standard object ordering commands (Forward One, Back One, etc.) can be used on a layer, affecting an object's level within the layer it currently occupies. For more information, see Ordering objects on p. 137.

At some point you may be confident that objects on separate layers can be managed on the same layer without compromising layer control. Merging layers enables this and will help to keep your layer management simpler. This rationalization is possible via the **Merge** button.

To merge a layer:

1.   Activate the layer you want to merge to by clicking its entry. The layer is highlighted in blue. (Note that the active layer becomes uppermost in the workspace.)

2.   With the **Ctrl** key pressed, select a single or multiple layers that you want to merge into the activated layer.

3.   Click the **Merge** button. The contents of the merged layer(s) appear on the active layer and the previously selected layers are removed.

If you're working on an especially complex document you can temporarily "freeze" a layer (and its objects).

Layer Properties

Layer properties allow you to assign paper textures, make layers invisible/visible, and/or locked/unlocked.

See Studio: Layers tab in DrawPlus Help for more details.

Managing objects on layers

A useful feature of the Layers tab is that you can see objects or even groups of objects, under the layer on which they were created. This gives you the option of selecting an object or group from the tab as opposed to from the page itself. Groups and individual objects can be named, allowing you to more easily locate them in the Layers tab, which in turn locates them in the workspace for you.

To add objects to a particular layer:

•   When drawn, objects are added to the selected layer automatically. This is why it is a good idea to check which layer you are currently working on!

To select objects on a particular layer:

- In the Layers tab, if the 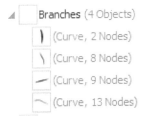 **Edit All Layers** button is disabled, click the chosen layer and either:

  - Click the layer's object on the page.
    - or -

  - In the Layers tab, click the ▶ **Expand** icon on the chosen layer entry to reveal all associated objects. You'll see objects named automatically, e.g. (Curve, 2 Nodes), (Closed Curve, 5 Nodes), (Quick Rectangle), etc., each with their own preview. The frontmost object in your drawing always appears at the top of the layer's listed objects (the order reflects the Z-order).

    Branches (4 Objects)

    | (Curve, 2 Nodes)

    \ (Curve, 8 Nodes)

    — (Curve, 9 Nodes)

    ⌒ (Curve, 13 Nodes)

    This tree view greatly improves the ability to select and manage nested objects in more complex drawings. It's also great for visualizing your object order.

To select any object on any layer:

Initially, objects which are on layers that are not selected are also visible, but you may find that you can't select an object as it is on a different layer. This can be slightly confusing at first as you frantically click on an object to no effect! But of course, you can change this state of affairs.

- If 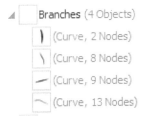 **View All Layers** is enabled (the default), all layers set as visible appear in the workspace, regardless of which layer you're currently working on. Disabling this button lets you see only objects on the current layer, as long as it's visible. (If both **Visible** and **View All Layers** are unchecked, you won't see anything!)

- If ✎ **Edit All Layers** (available only if **View All Layers** is enabled) is disabled (the default), you can only select objects in the current layer. Enabling this button lets you select any object on any visible layer.

- If ⬚ **Auto-Select Layer** is enabled (available only if **Edit All Layers** is enabled), you'll automatically select an object's layer and the object entry in the Layers tab as you select it on the page. This stops you from having to jump back to the Layers tab to set the layer to be active aYou can press the **Tab** key repeatedly to cycle between objects on the current layer (or across all layers if **Edit All Layers** is enabled).

To change an object or group name:

1. In the Layers tab, expand the layer entry to which an object or group belongs.

2. Select the object/group, then click on its name.

3. At the insertion point, type a new name then either press **Enter** or click away from the tab.

> 🖋 Trouble locating your **named** object or group? Search for it by using **Find Object...** on the **Edit** menu.

To move an object to another layer:

- Right-click the object in the workspace, and choose **Move Object to Layer...**. From the **Move To Layer** dialog, select the specific destination layer, and click **OK**.
  - or -

- Right-click the object in the workspace, and choose **Move Object to Active Layer**. The object moves to whichever layer was previously active.

8 Fill, Lines, Colours, and Transparency

Setting fill properties

Any closed shape, such as a closed curve or QuickShape, or text has an interior region that can be filled. The fill type can be solid, gradient, bitmap or plasma. Those that use a single colour are solid fills. Let's take a moment to run through them.

Fill types fall into several basic categories, illustrated above:

- **Solid fills**, as their name implies, use a single colour.

- **Gradient fills** provide a gradation or spectrum of colours between two or more "key" colours. Mesh fills work like gradient fills but with a more complex fill path.

- **Bitmap** and **Plasma fills** apply bitmapped images or patterns to the object, each with unique properties. Think of bitmap fills as named "pictures" that fill shapes. Plasma (or "fractal") fills use randomized patterns, useful for simulating cloud or shadow effects.

Solid colours

Applying a fill is easy, whether you're selecting a colour from the **Colour tab** or the **Swatch tab**.

The Colour tab can operate in several modes available from a drop-down list— HSL Colour Wheel (shown), HSL Colour Box, HSL Sliders, RGB Sliders, RGB Sliders (Hex), CMYK Sliders and Tinting.

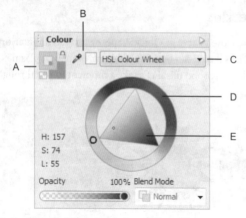

(A) Line/Fill swatches, (B) Colour Picker, (C) Colour Model, (D) Hue wheel, (E) Saturation/Lightness triangle.

On the HSL Colour Wheel, the small circles shown in the wheel and triangle indicate the current setting for hue and saturation/lightness, respectively. Drag either circle around to adjust the values.

The Line/Fill swatches on the tab govern whether the selected colour is applied as a line colour, solid fill, or both simultaneously.

By comparison, the Swatch tab hosts a vast array of preset colour swatches for solid, gradient, plasma, and bitmap fills. Swatches are stored in palettes which can be managed from within the tab. You can even create your own palettes and palette categories.

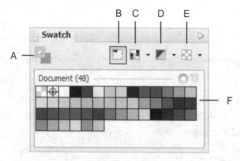

(A) Line/Fill swatches, (B) Document Palette, (C) Standard and themed palettes, (D) Gradient palettes, (E) Bitmap palettes, (F) Current palette.

CMYK operation

If you intend to create professional CMYK output to PDF or image, you can optionally create a CMYK drawing from scratch (see p. 23). Your drawing, in a CMYK colour space, can be designed using CMYK colours (instead of RGB colours) either using:

- **CMYK Sliders**. (Click the Colour Model drop-down list on the Colour tab.)

  - or -

- **Standard CMYK Palette**. (Click the Palettes button on the Swatch tab.)

Applying colour

To apply a solid fill colour via the Colour tab:

1. Select the object(s) and display the Studio's **Colour tab**.

2. Set the Line/Fill Swatch at the top-left of the tab so the Fill Swatch appears in front of the Line swatch.

This defines where the colour will be applied. Alternatively, apply colour to both line and fill simultaneously by clicking  **Link** on the swatch.

3. (Optional) Choose a colour display mode from the drop-down menu.

HSL Colour Wheel ▼
HSL Colour Wheel
HSL Colour Box
HSL Sliders
RGB Sliders
RGB Sliders (Hex)
CMYK Sliders
Tinting

4. Select a colour from the display.

To apply a solid fill colour via the Swatch tab:

1. Select the object(s) and display the Studio's **Swatch tab**.

2. Set the Line/Fill Swatch at the top-left of the tab so the Fill Swatch appears in front of the Line Swatch.

3. Pick a thumbnail from either the **Document Palette** or from another palette shown in the **Palettes** drop-down list (drag from the thumbnail onto the object as an alternative).

A **Tinting** option in the Colour tab's drop-down list allows a percentage of shade/tint to be applied to your colour.

To change a fill's shade/tint (lightness):

1. Select the object and set the Line/Fill Swatch as described for the Colour tab above.

2. From the tab's colour mode drop-down list, select **Tinting**.

3. Drag the slider to the left or right to darken or lighten your starting colour, respectively (the original colour is set at 0%).

You can also enter a percentage value in the box (entering 0 or dragging the pointer back to its original position reverts to the original colour).

To apply a gradient, bitmap, or plasma fill to one or more objects:

As for applying a solid colour fill with the Swatch tab but:

- Instead of using a solid colour palette, pick a relevant category from the **Gradient** or **Bitmap** galleries, and pick your required thumbnail from the displayed presets (drag from the thumbnail onto the deselected object as an alternative).

For solid, gradient or plasma fills, you can then edit **colour(s) and shade/tint** (lightness). For gradient and plasma fills, the fill **path** (coverage) can also be edited (see Working with gradient fills on p. 159).

To edit an object's fill colour(s) and tint:

1. Right-click the object and choose **Format>Fill...**.

2. (Optional) From the dialog's **Model** drop-down menu, choose a different colour model (e.g., RGB sliders).

3. Depending on the selected colour mode, use the Colour Wheel, Colour Picker, or combination of slider and colour spectrum (or use the input boxes) to set your colour value. When using the colour spectrum, click anywhere in the window then drag the marker around to fine-tune your colour selection.

4. Click **OK**.

> 🐾 An **Opacity** level can be applied to your fill at the same time that a colour is applied; this leads to powerful colour/opacity combinations on solid fills, or on gradient and plasma fill paths. (See Setting opacity on p. 166.)
>
> For gradient or bitmap transparency effects (see p. 170), use the Transparency Tool or Transparency tab.

> 💡 Exact colour values can be set in a **Colour Selector** dialog available by either double-clicking a Colour tab's swatch or from **Format>Fill...**.

To apply no fill:

Set an empty interior for objects by using the:

- **Colour tab**: Click ⬜ **No Fill** in the bottom-left corner of the Line/Fill Swatch.

  - or -

- **Swatch tab**: Choose the first swatch, ⬜ **None**, from any gallery.

Blend modes

The Colour tab hosts a **Blend Mode** drop-down list for blending overlapping object colours together in various ways. You'll find blend modes described in detail in Understanding blend modes on p. 164.

Setting line properties

All lines, including those that enclose shapes, have numerous properties, including colour, style, line ends, width, join (corner), and cap (end).

Using the Studio's Line tab, you can adjust **plain line** properties for any freeform, straight, or curved line, as well as for the edge of a shape, image or artistic text.

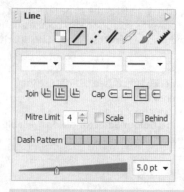

> To change line colour, see Setting fill properties on p. 147.

Changing line style

A series of buttons arranged along the top of the Line tab set the line style.

No line, **Solid**, **Dash**, **Double**, and **Calligraphic** styles can be applied to freeform lines, and outlines of shapes, images and artistic text alike.

The additional two line effects, **Brush Stroke** and **Edge Effect,** let you apply a brush (stroke, spray or edge) effect to the outlines of artistic text, images or objects. You can see your current brush in the Line tab and select a new brush from the Brushes tab. **Brush Stroke** styles can also be added to freeform lines.

To change line style:

- Simply click a button to set the line style—only one style can be set any one time. Pick another button to jump to that style.

Once a style is selected you can choose line ends for most styles (except Brush Stroke and Edge Effect). For some styles, variations are also available. For example, for a Dash or Double line style, additional dash patterns (below) and double line options can be selected.

To select a line end:

- From the drop-down menus, pick a line start and end.

Other styles such as Dash and Calligraphic offer further customization of the chosen style.

Changing line caps and joins

The Line tab also lets you vary a line's **Cap** (end) and the **Join** (corner) where two lines intersect. Both properties tend to be more conspicuous on thicker lines; joins are more apparent with more acute angles.

Changing line width

On a selected line, curve, or shape (opposite), drag the **Width** slider in the Line tab. To turn off the line, set the box to 0pt.

Sampling colours

Use the **Colour Picker** tool to sample (and then reuse) a colour from anywhere on your computer screen. The picked colour can then be made the current line or fill colour in DrawPlus.

Various sampling methods can be used depending on the type of object fill or screen area to be sampled.

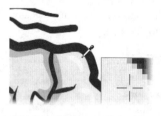

Point sampler
Use for picking up an individual pixel colour directly under the cursor.

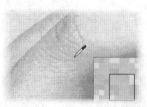

Square/circle sampler
Use for sampling halftone images, dithered GIFs, or images with undesirable colour artefacts. The colours within the shaped black outlined region in the magnification area are **averaged**, rather than using a specific pixel colour.

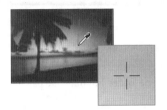

Gradient sampler
Use for picking up colour gradients present in images. Great for sampling colours in sunsets.

💡 Use the Colour tab's 🖋 **Colour Picker** to sample colours anywhere on your computer screen—click, hold the mouse button down, drag to the target area, and then release.

To sample colours:

1. On the **Drawing** toolbar, click 🖋 **Colour Picker**.

2. From the context toolbar, choose a colour picker type (e.g., Point Sampler).

   If you use the Square or Circle Sampler, set a **Colour Picker Size** appropriate to the area you want to sample. The Gradient Sampler offers a **Gradient Picker Sensitivity** option, for controlling the level or detail to which the gradient is sampled.

3. Hold the mouse button down, and drag to the target area then release. For gradient sampling, rather than clicking, you sample by dragging a line across your chosen colour gradient.

   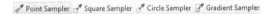 The sampled colour(s) is picked up in the Colour tab's **Picked Colour** swatch.

4. Click the Colour tab's **Line** or **Fill** swatch, then the Picked Colour swatch to transfer the colour to the chosen swatch. You can then apply the colour to any object (this will then be stored automatically in the Swatch tab's Document Palette for further use).

Defining line and fill colours

When you're applying a **fill** or **line colour** using the Studio's Swatch tab, you choose a colour from one of several colour **palettes**, arranged as a gallery of colour swatch thumbnails. Different palettes can be loaded but only one palette is displayed at any one time.

Several of the colour palettes are based on "themed" colours while the remaining palettes are based on industry-standard colour models, i.e.,

- **Standard RGB**: Red, Green and Blue (default).

- **Standard CMYK**: Cyan, Magenta, Yellow and Black. (For professional PDF or image printing, optionally from a CMYK drawing.)

Applying a colour from any of the above palettes to an object will add that to DrawPlus's **Document Palette**, a set of colours currently in use (or previously used) in your document (plus standard colours). The Document Palette is primarily used to reuse colours already in your document—great for working to a specific "tailored" set of colours.

To complement the default standard colours (**A**) in the Swatch tab's Document Palette, you can also store other palette colours (**B**), bitmap fills (**C**), gradient/plasma/mesh fills (**D**), and colour spreads (**E**).

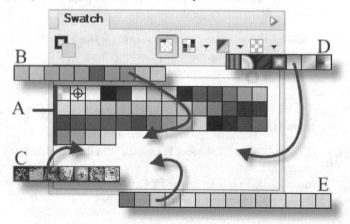

Adding colours to the Document Palette

Colours are added manually or automatically from the Colour tab or taken directly from an object's line/fill into the user's **Document Palette**.

The palette also stores commonly used colours (e.g., Red, Green, Blue).

Colours can be added, edited, deleted, or renamed within the Document Palette as in any of the other Swatch tab's palettes.

Colours in the Document Palette are just saved locally, along with the drawing's current defaults. That is, the colours don't automatically carry over to new drawings. However, changes to the other palettes are saved globally, making them available to all drawings.

To add a colour to the Document Palette (from Colour tab):

- Select a colour mixed from the Colour tab.

If the colour doesn't already exist in the Swatch tab's Document Palette, a new thumbnail appears for it.

To add a new colour (via dialog):

1. Display the Document Palette on the Swatch tab.

2. Click Palette Menu and select **Add New Colour....**

   - or -
   right-click any thumbnail and choose **Add....**

3. (Optional) From the **Colour Selector** dialog's **Model** drop-down list, choose a different colour model (e.g., CMYK sliders).

4. Depending on the selected colour mode, use the Colour Wheel, or combination of slider and colour spectrum (or use the input boxes) to set your colour value. When using the colour spectrum, click anywhere in the window then drag the marker around to fine-tune your colour selection.

5. Click **OK**. A new swatch is added to the palette.

> Use the **Colour Picker** in the Colour Selector dialog to sample colours from anywhere on your computer screen.

To add a colour to the Document Palette:

1. Select a different palette (themed, gradient, or bitmap palette).

2. Right-click a palette swatch and select **Add to Document's Palette**.

To add colour spreads (using Colour Palette Designer):

1. Click ⭕ **Colour Palette Designer** on the Document Palette's title bar.

2. Choose a **Base Colour**, a **Spread** (from the drop-down list), and click either the **Add Range** or **Add All** button.

3. Click **OK**.

For more details, see Creating colour palettes from spreads in DrawPlus Help.

To modify or rename a palette swatch:

•   Right-click the swatch and choose **Edit....**

To delete a palette swatch:

•   Right-click the swatch and choose **Delete....**

If any existing objects use the fill, if you delete it, the objects will retain it.

Adding fills to the Document Palette

To add a solid colour, gradient, mesh, or plasma fill (from a selected object):

1. Click ▽ **Palette Menu** and select **Add Fill from Selection**.

2. In the dialog, choose a name and click **OK**.

To add a bitmap fill (from an imported picture):

1. Click ▽ **Palette Menu** and select **Add Bitmap Fill....**

2. In the dialog, navigate to the bitmap, select the file name, and click **Open**.

Working with gradient fills

Gradient fills are those that use gradients—small "spectrums" with colours
spreading between at least two defined **key** values. Specifically, gradient fills
include the **Linear**, **Radial**, **Elliptical**, **Conical**, **Square**, **Three Colour**, and **Four
Colour** types. Once you've applied a gradient fill to an object using the Swatch
tab (see Setting fill properties on p. 147), you can use the **Fill Tool** to edit the
object's **fill path**, defining the placement of the spectrum across the object.

Applying a gradient fill

There are several ways to apply a gradient fill as a line colour or object fill: using
the Fill Tool or via the Swatch tab. Using the Fill Tool, you can vary the fill's path
on an object for different effects.

To apply a gradient fill (Fill Tool):

1. Select a coloured object.

2. Click the Swatch tab and ensure the [icon] **Line** or **Fill** swatch is set
   accordingly.

3. Click the [icon] **Fill Tool** on the **Drawing** toolbar.

4. Click and drag on the object to define the fill path (a solid line). The
   object takes a simple Linear fill, grading from the current colour of the
   object, ending in white (objects filled with white will grade from white
   to black, to show contrast).

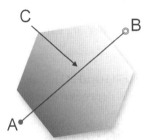

(**A**) Node (Start key colour),
(**B**) Node (End key colour), and
(**C**) Fill Path

To apply a gradient fill (Swatch tab):

1. Select an object.

2. Click the Swatch tab and ensure the ◻ **Line** or **Fill** swatch is set accordingly.

3. Select the ◢ ▾ **Gradient** button's drop-down menu and pick a gradient category.

4. Click the thumbnail for the fill you want to apply.
   - or -
   Drag from the gallery swatch onto any deselected object.

Editing the fill path

If an object using a gradient fill is selected, you'll see the **fill path** displayed as one or more lines, with circular nodes marking where the spectrum between each key colour begins and ends. Adjusting the node positions determines the actual spread of colours between nodes. You can also edit the fill by adding, deleting, or changing key colours.

To adjust the gradient fill path on a selected object:

1. Select an object with a gradient fill.

2. Click ◈ **Fill Tool** on the **Drawing** toolbar. The object's fill path appears.

3. Use the Fill Tool to drag the start and end circular path nodes, or drag on (or outside) the object for a new start node, creating a new fill path as you drag. The gradient starts where you place the start node, and ends where you place the end node.
   - or -
   Use the Fill context toolbar to change **Fill Start/Fill End** colours or **Rotate Left/Rotate Right** your fill (in 90 degree increments).

> ♀ To constrain the fill path in 15-degree increments, hold down the **Shift** key while dragging. On Elliptical fills, **Ctrl**-constraining also forces the gradient's aspect ratio to match the object's bounding box.

Each gradient fill type has a characteristic path. For example, Radial fills have single-line paths, with the gradient initially starting at the object's centre. Elliptical fills likewise begin at the centre, but their paths have two lines so you can adjust the fill's extent in two directions away from the centre. Radial fills are always evenly circular, while Elliptical fills can be skewed in one direction or another.

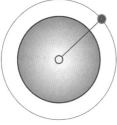

Radial Fill

Elliptical Fill

Experiment to discover new effects! For example, you can widen or narrow the gradient's extent, even drag either node completely outside the object. Or, for a Radial fill on a round shape, try placing the start node near the figure's upper edge, off-centre, to create a reflection highlight.

For details of how to edit and manage gradient fills, see DrawPlus Help.

Editing the fill spectrum

Whether you're editing a fill that's been already been applied to an object, or redefining one of the gallery fills, the basic concepts are the same. Whereas solid fills use a single colour, all gradient fills utilize at least two "key" colours, with a spread of hues in between each key colour, creating a "spectrum" effect.

You can either edit the fill spectrum directly using the **Fill Tool** or use **Format>Fill** (to access the Gradient Fill Editor dialog). With the Fill Tool selected, colours can be selected from the Studio's Colour or Swatch tab to replace a selected node's colour, or dragged from the Swatch tab to create new nodes on the fill path). Both methods let you define key colours. The Fill Tool method is more convenient for this, but with the dialog you can also fine-tune the actual spread of colour between pairs of key colours.

The editing of gradient fills is a complex operation and is covered in greater detail in the DrawPlus Help.

Working with bitmap and plasma fills

A **bitmap fill** uses a named bitmap—often a material, pattern, or background image. DrawPlus supplies an impressive selection of preset bitmap fills on the Swatch tab, and you can import your own.

A **plasma fill**, sometimes called a fractal fill, is a bitmapped pattern with dark and light regions, useful for simulating cloud or shadow effects. Again, the Swatch tab hosts a selection of these fills.

Once you've applied either type of fill to an object using the Swatch tab (see Setting fill properties on p. 147), you can adjust the fill's tint with the Shade/Tint slider in the Colour tab (use Colour mode drop-down menu), and use the Fill Tool to edit the object's **fill path**, defining the placement of the fill across the object.

Editing the fill path

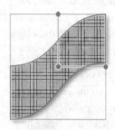

If an object using a bitmap fill is selected, you'll see the **fill path** displayed as two lines joined at a centre handle. Nodes, shown as small filled circles, mark the fill's centre and edges.

To reposition the fill's centre, drag the centre handle. To create a skewed or tilted fill region, drag one or both edge nodes sideways.

Unlike the other fill types, bitmap and plasma fills don't simply "end" at the edges of their fill path. Rather, they **tile** (repeat) so you can fill indefinitely large regions at any scale. By dragging the edge nodes in or out with the Fill Tool, you can "zoom" in or out on the fill pattern.

Edge nodes dragged outwards   *Edge nodes dragged inwards*

For details of how to edit and manage bitmap and plasma fills, see DrawPlus Help.

Working with mesh fills

A **mesh fill** works like a gradient fill but uses a more complex fill path, with a grid or "mesh" of many nodes representing separate key colours. The overall effect, especially useful for multifaceted highlighting, arises from the colour gradients that spread between each of these nodes.

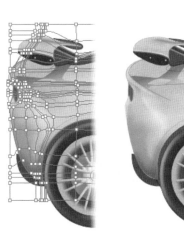

As an example, the **Mesh Fill Tool** can be used to dramatic effect on a sports car's bodywork.

To enable the Mesh Fill Tool:

- Select 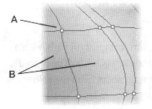 **Mesh Fill Tool** on the **Drawing** toolbar's Fill flyout. With the tool enabled, a mesh of editable patches and nodes are revealed (above).

A mesh fill is applied to an object via the Swatch tab's Gradient gallery (see Setting fill properties on p. 147). You can edit the mesh itself with the Mesh Fill Tool and the accompanying context toolbar to achieve unique results. The path lines that connect nodes in a mesh fill are actually curves, so editing the mesh is similar to the method for Editing lines and shapes (see p. 68). Simple warping effects, colour spread changes and path line curvature can all be affected. The tool lets you reshape curved path lines by adjusting one or more nodes and their control handles. In addition, the areas between four nodes called "mesh patches" can be recoloured or moved individually or in multiples. As for curved lines you can add, delete, and move one or more nodes at any time.

*(A) Node and
(B) Patches in a mesh fill*

Understanding blend modes

You can think of **blend modes** as different rules for combining pixels to create a resulting colour. Note that blend modes work in relation to the colours of the objects themselves (shapes, lines, brush strokes, and so on).

They are used for **creative effects** on overlapping objects, where colours blend on top of one another. Blend modes can be applied to both a top object's line and fill colour. You can adjust the blend mode of an existing object (brush stroke, etc.) on your page, or you can set the blend mode before creating a brush stroke, line, shape, etc.

For professional design, you can make use of **composite blend modes** or **isolated blending** within a group to prevent underlying objects from being affected by the blending operation.

To apply a blend mode to an existing object:

1. Select an existing object on your page.

2. On the **Colour** tab, choose a blend mode from the **Blend Mode** drop-down list.

To apply a blend mode to a new brush stroke, line, or shape:

1. Select the brush, line, or shape tool you want to use, and set its appropriate settings—width, colour, etc.

2. On the **Colour** tab, choose a blend mode from the **Blend Mode** drop-down list.

3. Create your stroke, line, or shape on your page.

Composite blend modes

When multiple objects are grouped (see p. 135), the group can be given a **composite blend mode**, which complements any blend mode applied to objects prior to being grouped. The composite blend is applied to the group after objects have been blended.

Composite blend modes are created by using the **Blend Mode** drop-down list on the Colour tab.

> If you ungroup, any blend modes set on any object before grouping will be reverted.

Using isolated blending

Blend modes applied to overlapping objects may inadvertently produce unwanted blending on underlying objects. This can be overcome by grouping blended objects, then isolating the blend effect within the group.

To apply isolated blending:

1. Select the grouped object containing blending.

2. From the context toolbar, check **Isolated Blending**.

Blend modes

The following table summarizes the blend modes available in DrawPlus.

- **Top colour** refers to the colour superimposed by an object's blend mode (the object may be a brush stroke, a shape, a photo, etc.).

- **Bottom colour** refers to the colour of the object onto which the top colour is applied (e.g., a background).

Setting opacity

> 💡 **Key point!** In DrawPlus, **opacity** is a property of colour, and can be set directly from the Colour tab. **Transparency** refers to object-based gradient or bitmap transparency effects, set via the Transparency tab or Transparency Tool.

Opacity is great for highlights, shading and shadows, and simulating "rendered" realism. It can make the difference between flat, ordinary visuals and sparkling realism!

Opacity is the inverse of transparency—fully opaque (100%) is no transparency (0%), and vice versa. It works rather like fills that use "disappearing ink" instead of colour. The less opacity in a particular spot, the more "disappearing" takes place there, and the more the object(s) underneath show through.

Butterflies showing 100% opacity, 50% opacity, and 25% opacity (left to right).

The **Opacity** slider (Colour tab) can be used to alter the opacity of a specific colour, whether that colour is a solid fill (in an object or on a line), or a node's colour on a gradient fill path. Opacity can be applied locally to each object; the default is 100% opacity, i.e., the object is fully opaque.

For solid fills, the opacity change will be made uniformly across the object's interior (as above). However, for gradient fill paths, different opacity levels can be assigned with colour to nodes along the fill path. The combination of different colours and semi-transparency allow interesting colour blends to be made.

> ✎ Gradient fill paths are explained in detail in Working with gradient fills on p. 159.

> ✎ Don't get confused between fill paths and transparency paths. The former is referred to here, but the latter is used to apply different levels of transparency along a transparency path instead of colour.

To apply solid opacity:

1. Select the object.

2. From the Studio's **Colour tab**, drag the slider to the left for a reduced **Opacity** setting (e.g., 20%); drag right to increase opacity. This makes objects appear semi-transparent, or if set to 0%, fully transparent.

To apply solid opacity (to a fill path):

1. Select the object with a gradient fill and display the Studio's **Colour tab**.

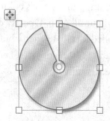

2. Click the  **Fill Tool** on the **Drawing** toolbar's Fill flyout. The fill path is displayed.

    Click on any displayed node along the fill path (the node with a double outline is selected. Use **Shift**-select for selecting multiple nodes.

3. From the Colour tab, drag the slider to the left for a reduced opacity setting. You'll notice the new opacity setting influencing the fill's appearance.

Composite opacity

An individual object can take a specific opacity setting. However, when multiple objects are grouped (see p. 135), the group can be given a **composite opacity**, affecting all group objects to the same extent. Composite opacity is possible by using the **Opacity** slider on the Colour tab.

Drawing without opacity

Result of objects selected individually, and assigned 50% opacity.

Result of objects grouped, with 50% ***composite opacity*** *applied to group.*

> ✎ Any opacity on objects prior to grouping will be honoured; composite opacity, when applied, will further increase the transparency of that object.
>
> ✎ If you ungroup, the opacity of the object before grouping is reverted to.

Knockout groups

When working with grouped semi-transparent objects you can use **knockout groups** to control how an object's colour and opacity interacts with an overlapping object's colour/opacity **in the same group**. When disabled (default), the "combined" colour/opacity is a blend of both objects. When enabled, the lower colours/opacity are "knocked out", i.e., replaced by the upper colours/opacity, avoiding potentially unwanted overlapping colour combinations.

For more information about grouping, see Grouping objects on p. 135.

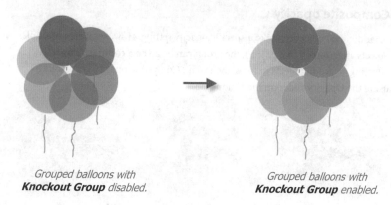

Grouped balloons with
Knockout Group *disabled.*

Grouped balloons with
Knockout Group *enabled.*

To create a knockout group:

1. Select the group (must contain overlapping objects).

2. From the context toolbar, check **Knockout Group**.

If you ungroup the group, you'll lose the knockout effect.

Using transparency effects

While uniform opacity can be applied along with colour via the Colour tab (see Setting opacity on p. 166), it's possible to apply gradient transparency via the Transparency tab or Transparency Tool independent of colour. Bitmap transparency can also be applied exclusively via the Transparency tab.

Just as a gradient fill can vary from light to dark, a gradient transparency varies from more to less transparency, i.e., from clear to opaque. Picking a linear transparency preset from the Transparency tab, and applying it to a shape, shows the transparency effect.

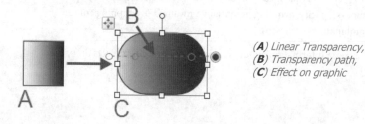

(A) Linear Transparency,
(B) Transparency path,
(C) Effect on graphic

Transparency can also be applied along a custom drawn transparency path using the Transparency Tool, in the same way as the equivalent fill path (see p. 160). Transparency paths are easily editable.

> Transparency effects are applied locally to each object. Applying different transparency effects won't alter the object's fill settings as such, but may significantly alter a fill's actual appearance.

Let's check out the Transparency tab. As with the Swatch tab, there are galleries for both gradient and bitmap transparencies.

Gradient transparency galleries include **Linear** (opposite), **Radial**, **Elliptical**, **Conical**, **Plasma**, **Square**, **Three Points** and **Four Points**, ranging from clear to opaque.

The **Bitmap** transparency gallery hosts texture maps based on the Swatch tab's selection of bitmaps.

Each preset's tooltip identifies its category.

To apply gradient or bitmap transparency effects:

1. With your object selected, go to the Transparency tab.

2. For gradient or bitmap transparency, click the drop down arrow on the **Gradient** or **Bitmap** button, respectively. Select a category from the flyout, then click a thumbnail in that category.
    - or -
    Drag the desired thumbnail from the gallery to an object.

3. The transparency is applied to the object(s).

> Sometimes objects of a lighter colour will not display their transparency clearly—ensure the transparency is applied correctly by temporarily placing the object over a strong solid colour.

To apply gradient transparency with Transparency Tool:

1. Select an object.

2. Click the  **Transparency Tool** on the **Drawing** toolbar.

3. Click and drag on the object to define the transparency path. The object takes a simple linear transparency, grading from 0% transparency (100% opaque) to 100% transparency (0% opaque) in the direction you drag.

   You have freeform control over where the path starts and ends, and the direction in which the path will be drawn. You can even click again to redraw the path.

Editing gradient transparency

Once you've applied a transparency, you can adjust its **path** on the object, and the **level** of transparency along the path. You can even create more complex transparency effects by adding extra nodes to the path and assigning different levels to each node.

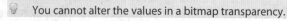

You cannot alter the values in a bitmap transparency.

To adjust the transparency path directly:

- Use the **Transparency Tool** to drag individual nodes, or click on the object for a new start node and drag out a new transparency path. The effect starts where you place the start node, and ends where you place the end node. For bitmap and plasma transparencies, the path determines the centre and two edges of the effect.

For details of how to edit and manage gradient transparency, see DrawPlus Help.

9 Working with Pictures

Importing pictures

Adobe PhotoShop Picture (*.psd)
GEM Raster Format (*.img)
GIF (*.gif)
JPEG (*.jpeg)
JPEG 2000 (*.j2k)
JPEG 2000 Compressed (*.jp2)
JPG (*.jpg)
Kodak Flash Pix (*.fpx)
Kodak Photo CD (*.pcd)
PaintBrush (*.pcx)
PhotoPlus Image (*.spp)
Portable Network Graphic (*.png)
PSP File (*.psp)
PSP Tube (*.tub)
TIFF (*.tif)
Truevision TARGA Format (*.tga)
Windows Bitmap (*.bmp)
Windows Enhanced Metafile (*.emf)
Windows Metafile (*.wmf)
Microsoft HD Photo (*.wdp,*.hdp)
Encapsulated Postscript (*.eps,*.ps)
Serif Metafile Format (*.smf)
Scalable Vector Graphics (*.svg)
Compressed Scalable Vector Graphics (*.svgz)

Pictures that can be imported into DrawPlus can belong to one of several groups:

- **Bitmapped** pictures, also known as **bitmaps** or **raster** images, are built from a matrix of dots ("pixels"), rather like the squares on a sheet of graph paper. They may originate as digital camera photos or scanned images, or be created (or enhanced) with a "paint" program or photo editor.

- **Vector** graphics, are resolution-independent and contain drawing commands such as "draw a line from A to B." These are like DrawPlus drawings, made of many individual objects grouped together, and you can edit them in the same sort of way. You have the choice of ungrouping the objects in order to edit them further, or leaving them as a group.

- **Metafiles** are the native graphics format for Windows (i.e., Windows MetaFiles) and combine raster and vector information. Serif also has its own metafile format, Serif MetaFile Format (SMF) , optimized for image sharing between Serif applications.

Any imported picture ends up as an object you can select, move, scale, shear, rotate—and even cut or crop using the **Knife** or **Crop Tool** on the **Drawing** toolbar. The Image Cutout Studio (p. 177) lets you cut the subject of your picture out from its background (and vice versa).

To import a picture from a file:

1. Click Insert Picture on the **Drawing** toolbar.

2. From the dialog, locate and select the file to import, then click **Open**. The dialog disappears and the mouse pointer changes to the Picture Size cursor. What you do next determines the initial size, placement, and aspect ratio (proportions) of the picture.

3. Either:

   - Insert the picture at a default size by simply clicking the mouse.
     - or -

   - Set the size of the inserted picture by dragging out a region and releasing the mouse button.

By default, the picture's aspect ratio is preserved. To allow free dragging to any aspect ratio, hold down the **Shift** key. To constrain the aspect ratio while scaling from the picture's centre as you drag, hold down the **Ctrl** key.

Notes:

- You can import **Serif PhotoPlus .spp** files directly into DrawPlus. The file is placed as a flattened bitmap.

- You can import photos directly from your camera's hard disk, which shows as a removable drive in Windows. However in advance of import, you may wish to back your photos up to your computer's hard disk, making them permanently available to your DrawPlus project.

- You can import scanner images via TWAIN Acquire (see p. 195).

- For importing from an inserted Kodak PhotoCD, choose **Picture>Photo CD...** from the **Insert** menu.

- Once placed, you can swap the picture by clicking **Replace Picture** on the context toolbar.

- You can always resize a picture after it has been placed by dragging its handles. For the finer points of resizing, see Resizing objects on p. 121.

- The Picture context toolbar appears automatically when you select an image on the page. Use the toolbar to quickly adjust **contrast**, **brightness**, **Red Eye,** or apply **Auto Level** or **Auto Contrast**.

  For more advanced **image adjustment** and **effect** filters, click the Picture context toolbar's **PhotoLab** button. See DrawPlus Help for further information.

- If you import an image with areas of transparency, you'll be able to manipulate the image's outline, i.e., convert to curves, apply line properties, effects.

Using Image Cutout Studio

Image Cutout Studio offers a powerful integrated solution for cutting objects out from their backgrounds. Depending on the make up of your images you can separate subject of interests from their backgrounds, either by retaining the subject of interest (usually people, objects, etc.) or removing a simple uniform background (e.g., sky, studio backdrop). In both instances, the resulting "cutout" image creates an eye-catching look for your design.

The latter background removal method is illustrated in the following multi-image example.

An initial image on a white background.

Cutout Studio "paints" transparency on the background. The tint indicates areas to be discarded.

Once cut out, a different image can be used as a more attractive background.

To launch Image Cutout Studio:

1. Select an image to be cut out.

2. Select ![cutout icon] **Cutout Studio** from the displayed Picture context toolbar. Image Cutout Studio is launched.

> Your original image, if linked, is unaffected in Image Cutout Studio. However, embedded images, when cut out, are altered permanently in the DrawPlus document.

Choose an output

It's essential that you choose an output type prior to selecting areas for keeping/discarding, either an alpha-edged or vector-cropped bitmap. The choice you make really depends on the image, in particular how well defined image edges are.

- **Alpha-edged Bitmap**: Use when cutting out objects with poorly defined edges. Transparency and pixel blending are used at the outline edge to produce professional results with negligible interference from background colours. The term "alpha" refers to a 32-bit image's alpha transparency channel.

- **Vector-cropped Bitmap**: Use on more well-defined edges. A cropped image with crop outline is created which can be later manipulated with the crop tools. You can optionally apply feathering and smoothness to the image edge; the background colour will not be removed.

To create an alpha-edged bitmap:

1. Select **Alpha-edged Bitmap** from the **Output Type** drop-down menu.

2. Drag the **Width** slider to set the extent to which the "alpha" blending is applied inside the cutout edge.

3. Adjust the **Blur** slider to smooth out the cutout edge.

To create a vector-cropped bitmap:

1. Select **Vector-cropped Bitmap** from the **Output Type** drop-down menu.

2. Drag the **Feather** slider to apply a soft or blurry edge inside the cutout edge.

3. Drag the **Smoothness** slider to smooth out the cutout edge.

4. The **Inflate** slider acts as an positive or negative offset from the cutout edge.

Selecting areas to keep or discard

A pair of brushes for keeping and discarding is used to enable parts of the image to be selected. The tools are called **Keep Brush** and **Discard Brush**, and are either used independently or, more typically, in combination with each other. When using either tool, the brush paints an area contained by an outline which is considered to be discarded or retained (depending on brush type). A configurable number of pixels adjacent to the outline area are blended.

 Either tool allows the default brush size to be set before you select areas for keeping/discarding. You can set your own custom size or use a small, medium, or large preset brush size. Choose from the top of the Studio workspace.

To aid the selection operation, several display modes are available to show selection.

  Show Original, **Show Tinted**, and **Show Transparent** buttons respectively display the image with:

- selection areas only

- various coloured tints aiding complex selection operations

- checkerboard transparency areas marked for discarding.

For Show tinted, a red tint indicates areas to be discarded; a green tint shows areas to be kept.

For Show transparent mode, a different **Background colour** can be set (at the bottom of the Studio) while Show Transparent is enabled; this may help give better contrast at cut edges while fine tuning.

To select image areas for keeping/discarding:

1.   In Image Cutout Studio, click either **Keep brush** or **Discard brush** from the left of the Studio workspace.

2.   (Optional) Pick a **Brush size** suitable for the area to be worked on.

3.   (Optional) Set a **Grow tolerance** value to automatically expand the selected area under the cursor (by detecting colours similar to those within the current selection). The greater the value the more the selected area will grow.

4.   Using the circular cursor, click and drag across the area to be retained. It's OK to repeatedly click and drag until your selection area is made—you can't lose your selection unless you click the **Reset** button. The **Undo** button reverts to the last made selection.

5.   If you're outputting an alpha-edged bitmap, you can refine the area to be kept/discarded within Image Cutout Studio (only after previewing) with Erase and Restore touch-up tools. Vector-cropped images can be cropped using standard DrawPlus crop tools outside of the Studio.

6.   Click   **OK** to create your cutout, or   **Cancel** to abort the operation.

> Make your outline edge as exact as possible by using brush and touch-up tools before committing your work.

You'll see your image on the poster page in its original location, but with the selected areas cut away (made transparent).

Autotracing

Instead of manually tracing a design, it's possible to automatically convert bitmaps back into vector objects by using **autotracing**. Its main function is for speedily reworking bitmapped **logos** (for further design modification), but its use is not confined to this. In fact, both greyscale and colour **photos** can equally be autotraced for eye-catching artistic effects.

For each of these uses, DrawPlus offers a studio environment and a specific preset profile which will produce optimum results while autotracing artwork of your chosen type. These profiles are called **Logo Image Trace**, **B/W Image Trace**, and **Photo Image Trace**.

- **Logo Image Trace**. For tracing of vector bitmaps (e.g., logos, signatures, or other designs with antialiasing).

- **B/W Image Trace**. For black and white tracings of photos, scanned images, and line drawings.

- **Photo Image Trace**. For colour tracing of photos.

The autotracing process is performed in a studio environment, which makes use of the above profiles. The studio gives the opportunity to preview before tracing, and customize chosen profile settings further to your liking. Most profile settings are unique to the profile.

To autotrace a selected image:

1. Click the drop-down arrow on the **AutoTrace** button (on context toolbar) and select a profile from the menu.
   - or -

   Click **AutoTrace** and choose a profile from the profile selection screen.

2. The AutoTrace studio appears with the original artwork displayed, along with adjustable sliders, a colour palette (logo profile only), or a collapsible preview window (photo profiles only) showing how your output will look once traced.

3. (Optional) Adjust the sliders at the right of the workspace (each unique to the profile used); your profile settings will be modified. If you want to save these modified settings you must save the changed profile to a new custom name.

4. Click 🌕 **Trace** to trace your logo, photo, or other bitmapped artwork. It's best to keep clicking this button to update your main window after any adjustment. If you want to abort the autotracing process, you can click the **Cancel** button on the progress bar.

5. (Optional) For fine-tuning your traced output, several options are possible:

    *   Click 🔧 **Adjust** to access **Merge**, **Fill**, and **Node tools** for fine-tuning your vector output.

    *   For removing colours in traced logo output, right-click on the palette colour you want to remove.

        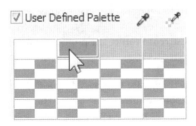

        You can **add** a new colour or **replace** an existing colour by left-clicking on an empty or occupied colour swatch and dragging the 🖌 **Colour Selector** to any colour on your computer screen. Remember to click **Trace** to refresh the view.

6. When you're happy with your traced output, click 🌕 **Accept** to add it to the page.

🠚 All slider settings are described in full in the Help pane which accompanies the AutoTrace studio. Also covered are procedures for tracing greyscale and colour photos.

The autotracing procedure above differs slightly when applied to greyscale or colour photos, i.e., instead of comprehensive palette control you have a photo preview.

Creating custom profiles

Adjusting any slider means that you've modified your chosen preset profile. If you want to keep the settings for future autotracing you can save the profile to a new name and reuse it from the drop-down menu (on the profile selection screen or within AutoTrace studio).

To save a custom autotrace profile:

1. Click ☆ **Save Current Profile**.

2. From the dialog, enter a custom profile name. The profile appears in the drop-down menu (in profile selection screen and studio).

To delete an autotrace profile:

1. Select the existing custom profile from the drop-down menu.

2. Click ✖ **Delete Current Profile**. The profile is removed from the menu.

> Use the upper **View** toolbar for side-by-side previews and different outline views. The zoom controls at the bottom of the studio offer magnification and panning control.

Cropping images

DrawPlus includes the **Crop Tool** which is used typically for cropping images (or vector outlines) on the page. Cropping discards unwanted "outer" regions of an object while keeping the remainder visible.

To crop an object:

1. Select an object and then on the **Drawing** toolbar, click the ☐ **Crop Tool**.

2. Click and drag an edge or corner handle towards the centre of the object.

As an aid, applying a **Rule of Thirds** grid helps the composition of your design during cropping.

To apply the Rule of Thirds:

1. Select your object and click the **Crop Tool**.

2. On the Crop context toolbar, click ⊞ **Show/Hide Thirds Grid**.

3. A 3 x 3 grid is superimposed on top of the object to aid cropping.

4. Drag a corner or edge grid handle to crop the image. As you do so, the grid repositions itself.

5. Manipulate the image to improve its framing.

-   Click and drag on the crop window to pan the image. For best results, aim to position your main subject of interest at a point where any two grid lines intersect, e.g. the eye.

- To rotate or zoom into or out of the object, use the adjacent control bar.

- Alternatively use equivalent button pairings on the context toolbar.

    $\oplus$ $\ominus$ **Zoom In/Out**

    $\circlearrowleft$ $\circlearrowright$ **Rotate anti-clockwise/clockwise**

- To select the crop window.

    Click **Back**, then select **Crop** from the control bar.

- To select cropped objects.

    Click **Back**, then click **Select Cropped Object(s)** from the control bar. The original object is selected.

- Uncrop a cropped area.

    Click **Uncrop** with the crop window selected.

- Crop an object using a preset shape.

    With the crop window selected, choose a QuickShape from the **Crop Shape** drop-down menu.

- To reshape a cropped area.

    With the crop window selected...

    1. Choose **Convert to Curves** on the **Arrange** tab.

    2. Select the **Node Tool**, then drag the window's **nodes**. For details, see Editing lines and shapes on p. 68.

Applying PhotoLab filters

PhotoLab is a dedicated studio environment that lets you apply adjustment and effect filters to photos, individually or in combination.

PhotoLab offers the following key features:

- **Adjustment filters**
  Apply White Balance, Lighting, Curves, Unsharp Mask, and an impressive selection of other corrective filters.

- **Effect filters**
  Apply distortion, blur, stylistic, noise, render, artistic, and various other effects for photo enhancement.

- **Retouching filters**
  Apply red-eye and spot repair correction.

- **Non-destructive operation**
  All filters are applied without affecting the original photo, and can be edited at any point in the future.

- **Powerful filter combinations**
  Create combinations of mixed adjustment, retouching, and effect filters for savable workflows.

- **Selective masking**
  Apply filters to selected regions using masks.

- **Save and manage favourites**
  Save filter combinations to a handy **Favourites** tab.

- **Viewing controls**
  Compare before-and-after previews, with dual and split-screen controls. Use pan and zoom control for moving around your photo.

- **Locking controls**
  Protect your applied filters from accidental change, then optionally apply them to other images on selection.

PhotoLab includes filter tabs, a main toolbar, and an applied filter stack around a central workspace.

Photos present in your drawing display in the **Images** tab, which is hidden by default. To display this tab, as illustrated below, simply click the ▲ button at the bottom of the dialog.

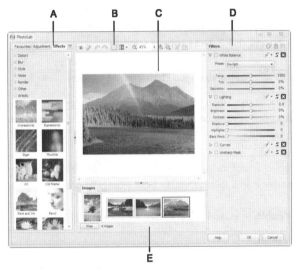

(A) filter tabs, (B) Main toolbar, (C) Main workspace, (D) filter stack, (E) Images tab

Filters are stored in the **Favourites**, **Adjustments**, and **Effects** filter tabs, and are grouped into categories.

For example, the **Adjustments** tab provides the **Quick Fix** and **Pro Edit** categories, while the **Effects** tab offers a wide range of creative effect categories.

On the **Favourites** tab, you'll find a selection of presets created with individual and combined filters. You can add your own custom filters to the **Favourites** tab. (See Saving Favourites on p. 194.)

When you apply a filter from one of these tabs, it is temporarily added to the **Trial Zone** that displays beneath the filter stack. This lets you preview and adjust filters before applying them.

Applying filters

1. 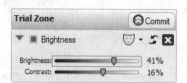 Select the photo you want to work on. (If the photo is framed, select it and click **Select Cropped Object**.)

2. Click 👁 **PhotoLab** on the Photo context toolbar.

3. For ease of use, when you open PhotoLab, the **Filters** stack on the right contains some commonly-used filters (such as **White Balance** and **Lighting**). These filters are disabled by default.

   To apply one of the default filters, click its ☐ **Enable/Disable** control to enable it, and then adjust the filter settings by dragging the sliders.

   To disable, reset, and delete a filter, see below.

To add a new filter:

1. Browse the filter thumbnails displayed on the **Favourites**, **Adjustments**, and **Effects** tabs, and click the one you want to apply.

   The selected filter is added to the **Trial Zone**, and the main window shows a preview of your photo with the filter applied.

Trial Zone	🔵 Commit
▼ ▪ Brightness	😊 ▾ ⟲ ❌
Brightness: ▬▬▬▬▬◻▭▭	41%
Contrast: ▬▬▬▬◻▭▭▭	16%

2. Experiment with the filter settings in the **Trial Zone**—you can drag the sliders, or enter values directly—to suit your requirements. (Note that some filters also offer check boxes, drop-down menus, and additional advanced controls.)

3. (Optional) To replace the trial filter, click a different thumbnail.

Selecting a new filter always replaces the current filter.

4. To apply the filter, click ⊖ **Commit** to add it to the **Filters** stack.

5. (Optional):

   • Repeat steps 1 to 4 to add more filters to the **Filters** stack.

     Filters are applied to a photo cumulatively, in the order in which they are added to the **Filters** stack. The most recently added filter always appears at the bottom of the stack. (See To reorder filters, below.)

   • Disable, reset, and/or delete filters in the **Filters** stack. (See below.)

   • Use zoom in/out buttons or a percentage magnification for detailed work.

   • Use the retouch tools to fix red eye and remove blemishes.

6. To apply all filters in the **Filters** stack and close PhotoLab, click **OK**.

To disable, reset, and delete filters:

   • To disable a filter, click ■ . Click ☐ to re-enable.

   • To reset filter values, click ↰ . Changes to settings revert to the filter's defaults.

   • To delete a filter, click ⊠ .

To reorder filters:

   • Drag and drop your filter into any position in the stack. A dotted line indicates the new position in which the entry will be placed on mouse release.

To add a filter directly (without trialling):

- Click 🔧 **Add Quick Filter** at the top of the **Filters** stack and choose a filter from the flyout categories. The filter is applied directly to the stack without being added to the **Trial Zone**.

Retouching

PhotoLab's main toolbar provides some useful retouching tools. These are commonly used to correct photos before applying colour correction and effects.

- 👁 **Red-eye tool**, to remove red eye from a human subject.

- 🩹 **Spot-repair tool**, to remove blemishes from human skin and material surfaces.

For instructions on using the retouching tools, see DrawPlus Help.

Selective masking

You may sometimes want to apply a filter to selected regions of a photo, rather than to the entire photo. In PhotoLab, you can do this by using a "mask" to define these region(s).

You can apply a mask:

- To the areas to which you want to apply the filter.

  - or -

- To the areas you want to protect from the filter.

  In the example below, a mask has been used to protect the subject of the photo from a **Stained Glass** filter effect.

To apply a mask:

1. From the  **Mask** drop-down menu, select **New Mask**.

2. In the **Tool Settings** pane, select the **Add Region** tool.

3. Adjust the settings to suit your requirements. For example, adjust **Brush Size** to paint larger or more intricate regions.

4. In the **Mode** drop-down menu, choose one of the following options:

   • **Select:** Choose this if you want to apply the filter only to the regions you paint. This is the default setting.

   • **Protect:** Choose this if you want to apply the filter to all areas of the photo, except for those that you paint.

5. Using the circular cursor, paint the regions to be masked (selected areas are painted in green; protected areas in red).

> If you've not been as accurate as you'd like while painting, click **Remove Regions** then paint over the unwanted painted regions.

6. Click ✅ to save your mask changes, or ❌ to cancel.

> The mask button changes to yellow when a mask is applied (i.e., ✏️).

You can create additional masks for the same filter, as above, and then choose between them. You can only apply one mask at any one time. By using the Mask menu's **New From>** option you can also base your new mask on an existing mask, which may be applied to the current filter or to any other filter in the stack. This is useful when working with **Favourites** filters that contain multiple adjustments.

To edit a mask:

- Expand the drop-down ✏️ Mask menu and select the mask you want to edit. Click **Edit Mask**.

Saving favourites

You can save specific filter settings, or combinations of filters, as favourites for future use.

PhotoLab stores all your favourites together in the **Favourites** tab. You can even create your own categories (e.g. My Adjustments) within the tab.

To save and manage favourites:

1. Click ![icon] **Save Filter**.

2. In the dialog, type a name for your filter and choose the category in which to save it.

    Click [···] to create a new category.

3. (Optional) To organize your favourites into user-defined categories, click the ▷ **Tab Menu** button and choose **Manage Favourites**.

Importing scanner images

In recent years, the increasingly more sophisticated image management software supplied with scanners means that DrawPlus leaves the photo management aspect of importing scanned images to the manufacturer's software (installed with the device on your computer). However, what DrawPlus offers is the ability to choose between different TWAIN sources, launch the manufacturer's software automatically, and subsequently place any chosen images onto the DrawPlus page.

To set up your digital device for image acquisition:

*   Follow the instructions supplied with the device.

To import pictures from a TWAIN device (i.e., scanner):

1. If you have multiple TWAIN-compatible devices, choose the device from which your image will be acquired—
    Picture>TWAIN>Select Source... from the **Insert** menu lets you select your device from a menu.

2. Choose **Picture>TWAIN>Acquire** from the **Insert** menu to open the device's image management dialog. Follow the device manufacturer's instructions, and select the scanned image for import.

3. In DrawPlus, the ![icon] Picture Size cursor is displayed which allows image to be placed at default size (by single-click) or sized (by dragging across the page).

You can also use the above procedure for importing photos from cameras that support TWAIN. More typically, modern cameras allow photo import (see p. 173) directly from their own memory cards, appearing as a removable disk in Windows.

10 Applying Special
Effects

Creating borders

The **Border Wizard** lets you create a border around the whole page or a selected object, or within a specific page region. It's possible to create your own border from a current object selection or from a preset border style.

To create a border:

1. (If creating a border around an object) Select the object first.

2. Select **Border Wizard...** from the **Insert** menu.

3. From the dialog, choose to select a border from a library of pre-designed borders (From library) or make your own border (based on the Current selection). Click **Next>**.

4. Choose where you want the border to be placed (e.g., around the current selection) and click **Next**.

5. For presets, choose one of the pre-defined border designs from the scrolling list, and set the border's width. If making your own border, enable a different border style. The preview window shows what the border will look like in both instances.

6. Click **Finish**.

If you chose a whole-page or object border, it appears immediately. With the "custom" option, use the cursor to drag out a region to be bordered.

> ❋ You can create a border on individual pages but not on all pages simultaneously.
>
> ❋ For edging effects, you can apply brush strokes or preset edges around your object. (See Changing line style on p. 153.)

Creating blends

Blends enable you to create shapes between two separate shapes on the page. These could be identical in shape but have different line/fill properties or be differently shaped. For the latter, the blending process "morphs" one shape into the other shape.

Each step creates an intermediate shape, where the colour, transparency, and line properties may all change, along with the object shape, during the blend process.

For same shapes:

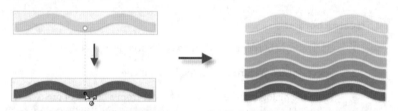

For different shapes (e.g. a blend between a Quick Ellipse and a Quick Petal):

> 💡 You can also "leap frog" between existing blends to create daisy-chained blends (by click and drag on each object consecutively).

To create a blend with the Blend Tool:

1. Select the 🖫 **Blend Tool** button on the **Drawing** toolbar.

2. (Optional) From the displayed Context toolbar, choose:

   - The number of "morph" **Blend Steps** to be taken between both points (to increase/decrease the smoothness of the blend).

- A Position Profile or Attribute Profile for non-uniform blends—use for rate or transform and blend, respectively. (See Using blend profiles.)

- A **Colour blend type** which defines how colour distribution occurs between the originating and destination object. You can **Fade** between colours by default, apply a **Clockwise/anti-clockwise** colour spread around the HSL Colour Wheel (from the Colour tab), or use the **Shortest** or **Longest** route between colours on the HSL Colour Wheel.

3. Hover over the object to display the Blend cursor.

🖈 If blending to multiple objects, remember to group them in advance.

4. Click and drag the cursor, drawing a dashed line as you go, to your destination point (this must be on an object) and release. Your blend is created.

5. (Optional) Click the 🖻 **Convert Blend Object into a Group Object** button on the context toolbar to group all blended objects.

🖈 ⊗ Any blend can be modified or removed via the context toolbar. To remove, use the **Remove blend on the current blend object** button.

Blending on a path

DrawPlus allows you to make your blended objects conform to a path, i.e. a drawn curve.

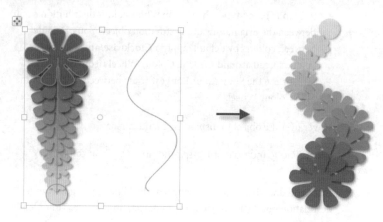

To fit a blend to a line or curve:

1.   Select the path (curve) and the previously blended object.

2.   From the **Tools** menu, select **Fit Blend to Curve**.

You'll be able to reshape the curve by manipulating its segments, on-curve nodes, and off-curve control handles. Individual nodes can also be assigned a different colour or transparency to change the blend appearance. (See Editing lines and shapes on p. 68).

Blends in Stopframe animation

For Stopframe animation of simple objects, you can make use of blending between objects to create frames automatically. You can perform this operation in Drawing mode (then **Convert to Stopframe Animation**) or from scratch in Stopframe Animation mode. See Stopframe animation tips and tricks in DrawPlus Help for more information.

Creating rough edges

The **Roughen Tool** lets you selectively distort an object's outline, turning smooth-line edges into jagged outlines. The effect can lend cartoon-like flair to ordinary text or give QuickShapes an irregular appearance, in fact apply it whenever it seems to suit the mood of the design.

To apply roughening:

1. Select an object and click the **Roughen Tool** on the **Drawing** toolbar's Transform flyout.

2. Click on the object and drag up or down. The further you drag, the more pronounced the effect.

Applying perspective

The **Perspective Tool**, like the Envelope Tool, produces an overall shape distortion. Perspective gives you the visual impression of a flat surface being tilted (or skewed) in space, with an exaggerated front/back size differential.

To apply a perspective effect:

1. Select an object and click **Perspective Tool** on the **Drawing** toolbar's Transform flyout. The **Node Tool** becomes the active tool and an adjustment slider appears above the object.

2. Drag the ⊹ "3D" cursor over the selected object or drag the special adjustment slider handle left or right to see it respond by tilting in all sorts of orientations. Use Undo if you're not happy with a particular adjustment.

   - or -

   From the context toolbar, select an item from the **Perspective Presets** flyout closest to the effect you're after. The first item, **User Defined perspective**, retrieves the last drawn custom perspective shape used in your current DrawPlus session. You can still use the cursor and handles for adjusting perspective.

Applying envelopes

An envelope distortion is one that you can apply to any object to change its shape without having to edit its nodes. You can use envelopes to bend text into a wave, arch, trapezoid, or just about any other shape. You can edit envelopes into custom shapes and apply them to other objects for corresponding effects.

With the **Envelope Tool**, an object's nodes can be moved in order to create custom envelopes or to allow preset envelopes to be applied to the selected object. The displayed context toolbar, shown while the tool is active, offers various options to customize the envelope—envelope shape, line colour, width, and style can all be altered. It also lets you pick from a range of pre-defined envelopes of various shapes, remove the selected object's envelope or apply curve adjustments on the envelope's boundary.

To apply an envelope:

1. Select the object(s) you want to be enveloped.

2. ⬜ ⬜▾ Click **Envelope Tool** on the **Drawing** toolbar's Transform flyout.

3. From the context toolbar, select an envelope preset from the **Preset Envelopes** flyout. The first item, User Defined envelope, retrieves the last drawn custom envelope shape used in your current DrawPlus session.

To remove an envelope:

*   Select the envelope with the **Envelope Tool**, then choose ⊗ **Remove Envelope** from the Envelope context toolbar.

To create/edit your own envelope:

*   Select the object(s) with the **Envelope Tool**.

*   Drag the nodes and handles accordingly.

DrawPlus automatically selects the **Node Tool** when an envelope is applied. The Node Tool along with the displayed curve buttons on the Envelope context toolbar lets you reshape the envelope by dragging its corner nodes and attractor nodes, as when editing curved lines. (To review these concepts, see Editing lines and shapes on p. 68.) The only difference is that you cannot add or delete corner nodes to an envelope. Envelopes always have exactly four line segments, one on each side.

Adding drop shadows

You can apply simple drop shadows by using the **Shadow Tool**. When applied, the selected object is given a sense of depth.

The **Shadow Tool** offers freeform control of the drop shadow effect. With its on-the-page control nodes and supporting Shadow context toolbar, the tool offers various adjustments such as Opacity, Blur, and X (or Y) Shear. Nodes appear on the object for fine control.

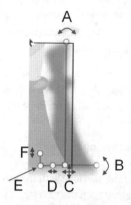

Simple shadow
(drag from object centre)

Node controls:
*(**A**) Shear X/Scale Y, (**B**) Shear Y/Scale X,*
*(**C**) Reposition shadow, (**D**) Opacity,*
*(**E**) Lock Point, (**F**) Blur.*
(showing control nodes)

With subtle Shear and Scale adjustments you can produce **skewed shadows** for realistic 2D lighting effects. The example opposite has had adjustments to Shear X and Shear Y, with blurring and reduced opacity.

Applying drop shadows with Shadow Tool

1. Click the 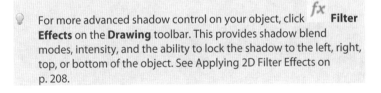 **Shadow Tool** on the **Drawing** toolbar. You'll notice control nodes appear which allow adjustment as described in the annotated illustration above.

2. Drag across the object to create a drop shadow (note additional nodes being created).

3. Change blur, opacity, shear, or scale accordingly by node adjustment (or via the displayed context toolbar).

> If you want to create simple shadows without additional control of the above properties, disable **Advanced** on the context toolbar, then drag the shadow to a new position.

To change a shadow's colour:

- Select a colour from the Studio's Colour tab.

To remove the shadow from an object:

- Double-click the object while the Shadow Tool is selected.

> For more advanced shadow control on your object, click *fx* **Filter Effects** on the **Drawing** toolbar. This provides shadow blend modes, intensity, and the ability to lock the shadow to the left, right, top, or bottom of the object. See Applying 2D Filter Effects on p. 208.

Applying 2D filter effects

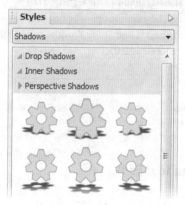

The Styles tab also offers an impressive selection of **preset 2D filter effects**, stored in various gallery categories (i.e., Shadows, Blurs, Bevels, Edges), further separated into subcategories.

> ✦ The tab also hosts some other styles unrelated to 2D filter effects.
>
> ✦ DrawPlus additionally provides the Shadow Tool for applying a shadow to an object directly on your page. Control handles let you adjust shadow blur, opacity and colour. See Adding drop shadows on p. 206.

To apply a preset effect:

1. Select an object.

2. From the Styles tab, select a category from the drop-down list.

3. Select a thumbnail in the chosen category. You may need to expand a subcategory by clicking ◢ **Expand**.

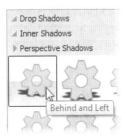

4. The effect is applied to the object.

Applying bevels and embossing effects

You can apply some depth to your objects by applying an embossing effect.

- From the Styles tab, adjust the **Bevel & Emboss** setting on your selected object. The greater the value, the greater the embossed effect.

Applying feathered edges

Feathering applies a softer edge to your objects, such as embellishments or cut materials. The effect is especially useful for presenting a photo on the page.

- From the Styles tab, pick a **Feather Edge** setting. This is the distance inside the object's outline within which feathering will be applied.

Advanced 2D filter effects

fx For more advanced control of filter effects, a **Filter Effects** dialog can be used to apply filter effects to an object. The following filter effect examples are possible via the dialog. Each effect is shown when applied to the letter "A."

Drop Shadow   Inner Shadow   Outer Glow   Inner Glow   Colour Fill

Inner Bevel   Outer Bevel   Emboss   Pillow Emboss   Feather

Gaussian Blur   Zoom Blur   Radial Blur   Motion Blur   Outline

To apply 2D filter effects:

1. Click *fx* **Filter Effects** on the **Drawing** toolbar. The Filter Effects dialog appears.

2. To apply a particular effect, check its box in the list at left.

3. To adjust the properties of a specific effect, select its name and vary the dialog controls. Adjust the sliders or enter specific values to vary the combined effect. (You can also select a slider and use the keyboard arrows.) Options differ from one effect to another.

5. Click **OK** to apply the effect or **Cancel** to abandon changes.

Creating outlines

DrawPlus lets you create a coloured outline around objects, especially text and shapes (as a **filter effect**). For any outline, you can set the outline width, colour fill, transparency, and blend mode. The outline can also take a gradient fill, a unique **contour** fill (fill runs from the inner to outer edge of the outline width), or pattern fill and can also sit inside, outside, or be centred on the object edge.

As with all effects you can switch the outline effect on and off. You'll be able to apply a combination of 2D or 3D filter effects along with your outline, by checking other options in the Filter Effects dialog.

Colour Fill

The **Colour Fill** effect applies a colour over any existing fill, and lets you achieve some effects that are not possible with other controls. For example, you can use Colour Fill to force everything in a complex group to a single colour, or recolour a bitmap in a solid colour (effectively ignoring everything but the transparency).

Feathering

Feathering is a filter effect that adds a soft or blurry edge to any object. It's great for blending single objects into a composition, vignetted borders on photos, and much more. You can apply feathering in conjunction with other filter effects.

Blur

Various blur effects can be applied to DrawPlus objects. The types of blur include:

- **Gaussian**: the effect smooths by averaging pixels using a weighted curve.

- **Zoom**: applies converging streaks to the image to simulate a zoom lens.

- **Radial**: applies concentric streaks to the object to simulate a rotating camera or subject.

- **Motion**: applies straight streaks to the object to simulate the effect of camera or subject movement.

Using 3D filter effects

3D filter effects go beyond 2D filter effects (shadows, bevel, emboss, etc.) to create the impression of a textured surface on the object itself. Keep in mind is that none of these 3D effects will "do" anything to an unfilled object—you'll need to have a fill there to see the difference they make!

The Studio's Styles tab is a good place to begin experimenting with 3D filter effects. Its multiple categories each offer a gallery full of predefined effects, using various settings.

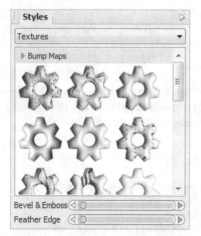

You'll see a variety of remarkable 3D surface (Glass, Metal, Wood, etc.) and texture presets in the Instant Effects and Textures categories, respectively. Click any thumbnail to apply it to the selected object. Assuming the object has some colour on it to start with, you'll see an instant result!

fx   Alternatively, you can customize a preset, or apply one or more specific effects from scratch, by choosing **Filter Effects** from the **Drawing** toolbar. If you want to keep the effect for future, you can save it.

To apply 3D Effects:

- Choose *fx* **Filter Effects** from the **Drawing** toolbar (or choose **Filter Effects...** from the **Format** menu, or right-click the object and choose **Filter Effects...**).

- Check **3D Effects** in the Filter Effects dialog.

- Adjust the "master control" sliders here to vary the overall properties of any individual 3D effects you select.

    - **Blur** specifies the amount of smoothing applied (in point size). Larger blur sizes give the impression of broader, more gradual changes in height.

    - **Depth** specifies how steep the changes in depth appear (in point size).

    - The ⊞ button is normally down, which links the two sliders so that sharp changes in Depth are smoothed out by the Blur parameter. To adjust the sliders independently, click the button so it's up.

- (Optional) If needed, expand the preview pane by clicking the ▷ **Show/Hide Preview** button. When expanded, the effects are applied only in the preview window. While the pane is collapsed (click the button again), filter effects are applied directly to the object on the page. The former approach lets you work on your effects in isolation without other page objects interfering while fine-tuning your effects. Use zoom in/out buttons or a percentage magnification for detailed work.

- Check a 3D effect in the 3D Effects list which reflects the 3D effect you can achieve.

3D Bump Map

The **3D Bump Map** effect creates the impression of a textured surface by applying a mathematical function you select to add depth information, for a peak-and-valley effect. You can use 3D Bump Map in conjunction with one or more additional 3D filter effects—but not with a 2D Bump Map. (See DrawPlus Help for background and technical details on these effects.)

2D Bump Map

The **2D Bump Map** effect creates the impression of a textured surface by applying a greyscale bitmap you select to add depth information, for a peak-and-valley effect. You can use 2D Bump Map in conjunction with one or more additional 3D filter effects—but not with a 3D Bump Map. (See DrawPlus Help for background and technical details on these effects.)

3D Pattern Map

The **3D Pattern Map** effect creates the impression of a textured surface by applying a mathematical function you select to introduce colour variations. You can use 3D Pattern Map in conjunction with one or more other 3D filter effects. (See DrawPlus Help for background and technical details on these effects.)

2D Pattern Map

The **2D Pattern Map** effect creates the impression of a textured surface by applying a greyscale bitmap you select to introduce colour variations. You can use 2D Pattern Map in conjunction with one or more other 3D filter effects.

Transparency

The uniform transparency of an object (with 3D filter effects applied) can be controlled via the Colour tab (see first example below). However, for more sophisticated transparency control, especially for simulating reflective lighting effects on glass objects, transparency settings can instead be set within the 3D filter effects dialog (check the **Transparency** option).

Transparency can be adjusted independently for both non-reflective surfaces (typically an object's edge shadows shown when side-lit) and top-lit surfaces (see second example below).

3D Reflection Map

The **3D Reflection Map** effect is used to simulate mirrored surfaces by selection of a pattern (i.e., a bitmap which possesses a shiny surface) which "wraps around" a selected object. Patterns which simulate various realistic indoor and outdoor environments can be adopted, with optional use of 3D lighting to further reflect off object edges.

3D Lighting

The **3D Lighting** effect works in conjunction with other 3D effects to let you vary the surface illumination and reflective properties.

Applying paper textures

Use **paper textures** for a natural "paper-like" appearance on your design. Simulate textures of varying roughness and "feel" by selection of various real media textures such as **Canvas**, **Cartridge**, **Embossed**, **Parchment**, and **Watercolour**. As a paper texture is applied to all objects on a specific layer you can apply different paper textures on a layer-by-layer basis.

To apply a paper texture:

1. In the Layers tab, decide on which layer you wish to apply a paper texture to its objects.

2. Click the **Paper Texture** button shown after that chosen layer's name and, from the dialog, select the **Paper Textures** category. A gallery of texture thumbnails is displayed.

3. Choose one of the thumbnails and adjust percentage **Scale** and **Opacity** if needed.

4. Click **OK**. The button will change, e.g. , to indicate that a paper texture has been applied. Existing or any subsequently new objects will adopt the paper texture once applied.

To remove a paper texture:

1. Click the button on the layer from which you want to remove a paper texture.

2. From the dialog, simply click the **Remove** button. The paper texture is removed from all objects on the layer.

You can also swap or remove paper textures from within the Layer Properties dialog (right-click on a layer entry and choose **Layer Properties...**).

Applying dimensionality (Instant 3D)

Using the **Instant 3D** feature, you can easily transform flat shapes (shown) and text into three-dimensional objects.

DrawPlus provides control over 3D effect settings such as:

- **Bevelling**: use several rounded and chiseled presets or create your own.

- **Lighting**: up to eight editable and separately coloured lights can be positioned to produce dramatic lighting effects.

- **Lathe effects**: create contoured objects (e.g., a bottle cork) with user-defined lathe profiles and extrusion control.

- **Texture**: control how texture is extruded on objects with non-solid fills.

- **Viewing**: present your object in three dimensions.

- **Material**: controls the extent to which lighting has an effect on the object's surfaces (great for 3D artistic text!).

An always-at-hand 3D context toolbar hosted above your workspace lets you configure settings—each setting contributes to the 3D effect applied to the selected object. For on-the-page object control you can transform in 3D with use of an orbit circle, which acts as an axis from which you can rotate around the X-, Y-, and Z-axes in relation to your page. Look for the cursor changing as you hover over either the circles' nodes or periphery.

X rotation   *Y rotation*   *Z rotation*   *X and Y rotation*

Remember to take advantage of the hover-over cursor text or hintline which indicate the object's rotation currently or rotation while the operation is in progress, respectively.

> ✦ Transform about your 3D objects' axes instead of your pages' axes by holding the **Ctrl** key down as you transform.

You can also adjust the angle and elevation of each "active" light on the page by dragging the light pointer to a position which simulates a light source.

To add dimensionality:

1. Select an object and click ⬦ **Instant 3D** on the **Drawing** toolbar.

   The object immediately adopts 3D characteristics with an orbit circle displayed in the object's foreground. You'll also notice a 3D-specific context toolbar appear above your drawing.

2. Click a 3D effect category from the first drop-down menu on the 3D context toolbar (from **Bevel**, **Lights**, **Lathe**, **Texture**, **Viewport**, **Material**); the other toolbars' options change dynamically according to the category currently selected. See DrawPlus Help for more details.

3. Set each drop-down menu or input box for each category in turn. A little experimentation is advisable.

4. Hover over the object's orbit circle and rotate about the X, Y or Z axis (or X and Y axes together) by dragging about the circle's periphery (depending on the currently displayed cursor).

To revert your Instant 3D transform:

- Click ↰ **Reset Defaults** on the context toolbar.

To switch off 3D effects:

- Click ⊗ **Remove Instant 3D** on the context toolbar. You can always select the object again then click the **Drawing** toolbar's **Instant 3D** button to reinstate the effect.

The Bevel and Lathe categories offer several presets that you can apply as your profile. You can also define your own custom profiles for both bevel and lathe effects from the Instant 3D context toolbar. (See DrawPlus Help for more details.)

For high-quality display, you can make DrawPlus display your Instant 3D objects at higher resolutions. Alternatively, the resolution can be reduced for quicker redrawing on slower computers.

To change Instant 3D display resolution:

- Select a resolution from the Display Resolution drop-down list in **Tools>Options...** (Drawing Quality>View Quality).

Applying Pseudo 3D

Pseudo 3D produces an object projection to follow one of three separate planes (top, front or right), either by using an **Isometric projection** (default) or other more complex projection. By bringing together transformed objects on each plane you produce the illusion of working in three dimensions, from a simple cube (below) to more complex 3D shapes, text, etc.

Each projection, from the same Quick Square object, can be presented as follows (with a combined multi-object cube).

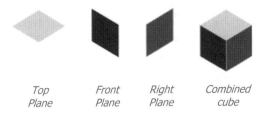

| Top Plane | Front Plane | Right Plane | Combined cube |

In DrawPlus, you can specify a plane (Top, Front, or Right) directly from the **Standard** toolbar's **3D Planes** flyout. While working with the toolbar all newly created objects will be drawn according to the currently set plane. Only one plane can be set at any one time.

For more complicated projections, DrawPlus also allows **Cabinet Oblique**, **Cavalier Oblique**, and various **Dimetric** and **Trimetric** projections to be applied; you can also design your own **Custom** projection. All projections represent a different object position about the X, Y and Z axes. Here's some simple cubes to illustrate a simple isometric projection compared to some more advanced projections.

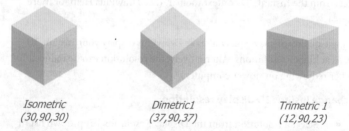

Isometric	Dimetric1	Trimetric 1
(30,90,30)	*(37,90,37)*	*(12,90,23)*

Notice how the displayed angles on each of the above projections are shown after each name.

 Practically, projection drawing can be challenging as it's sometimes difficult to visualize objects that appear three dimensional. To aid drawing, you can use the snapping grid which shows automatically in the page background; the grid intelligently switches to the current plane that you're working on. Whichever plane is set, drawn objects will then snap to the grid on the same plane.

To apply a Pseudo 3D projection:

1.   From the **Standard** toolbar, click 3D Planes, then select **Top Plane**, **Front Plane**, or **Right Plane** to set the plane to work on. (You'll see the snapping grid appear which reflects the currently set plane.)

2.   Click a drawing tool and drag out the object (e.g., a Quick Rectangle) on the plane (an isometric projection is created by default).

3.   All subsequently drawn objects are projected onto the currently set plane, unless it is swapped to a different plane (select a different button and draw a new object).

If this step-by-step process is followed, it's possible to bring together projected objects to create a larger object which simulates 3D characteristics.

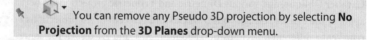 You can remove any Pseudo 3D projection by selecting **No Projection** from the **3D Planes** drop-down menu.

From the same drop-down menu, **Switch Plane on Select** can be disabled to stop automatically switching to the plane of a projected object when selected.

If you're creating a large number of objects, all on different planes, you can select all objects which project onto the same plane—useful for changing the colour of object faces for instance.

Selecting objects on the same plane:

- From the **Select All On Plane** option on the **Edit** menu, choose **None**, **Top**, **Front**, or **Right** from the menu.

To project an object to a different plane:

- Select a previously projected object, and with the **Ctrl** key depressed, choose a different plane from the **3D Planes** drop-down menu.

Using Advanced Pseudo 3D

Up to now we've assumed that you've applied a default isometric projection. However, DrawPlus can create other axonometric projections by changing the current Projection Properties (from drop-down menu) before drawing objects.

To apply an advanced Pseudo 3D projection:

1. Click **Projection Properties** on the 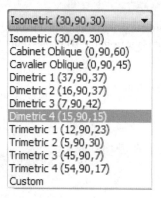 3D Planes drop-down menu.

2. From the dialog, select a projection type from the drop-down list.

```
Isometric (30,90,30)         ▼
Isometric (30,90,30)
Cabinet Oblique (0,90,60)
Cavalier Oblique (0,90,45)
Dimetric 1 (37,90,37)
Dimetric 2 (16,90,37)
Dimetric 3 (7,90,42)
Dimetric 4 (15,90,15)
Trimetric 1 (12,90,23)
Trimetric 2 (5,90,30)
Trimetric 3 (45,90,7)
Trimetric 4 (54,90,17)
Custom
```

Creating a custom projection:

•   From the **Projection Properties** dialog, pick a preset projection, and modify **Angle** and/or **Scale** values for one or more axes. The projection's name changes to **Custom**.

Saving a custom projection:

1. Click 🖫 **Save**.

2. In the dialog enter a name for the new projection and click **OK**. The entry will appear at the end of the drop-down menu.

11 Creating Animations

Getting started with animation

What is animation? Like flip books, Disney movies, and TV, it's a way of creating the illusion of motion by displaying a series of still images, rapidly enough to fool the eye—or more accurately, the brain. Professional animators have developed a whole arsenal of techniques for character animation—rendering human (and animal) movement in a convincing way.

A clear distinction has to be made between two types of animation techniques, both possible from within DrawPlus, i.e.

- **Stopframe animation**: also known as Stop motion animation, involves the animation of static objects frame-by-frame. In the film industry, Stopframe animation is used within widely known productions based on figures made of clay or other bendable material—think King Kong!, and more recently Wallace & Gromit™ films (Aardman/Wallace and Gromit Ltd).

- **Keyframe animation**: performs movement of computer-generated objects from basic shapes to cartoon characters (used traditionally in Stopframe animation). Using the power of computing, smooth playback of animated objects is easily achieved between key moments in your animation, defined by the user as **Keyframes**.

DrawPlus lets you export Stopframe or Keyframe animations to a variety of different formats. For more details, review Exporting animations (see p. 248).

For now we'll look at how to set up both Stopframe or Keyframe animation within DrawPlus.

To begin a new Stopframe or Keyframe animation (from Startup Wizard):

1. Start DrawPlus (or choose **File>New>New from Startup Wizard...** if it's already running).

2. Select **Create>Stopframe Animation** or **Create>Keyframe Animation** from the Startup Wizard.

3. From **Page Setup**, review document types in the left-hand pane.

4. Select a document type thumbnail from a category in the left-hand pane.

5. (Optional) For custom settings, from the right-hand of the dialog, click a **Paper** or **Animation** properties setting and either choose a different drop-down list option or input new values to modify. Typically, you can change Width, Height, and Orientation settings in the **Paper** category.

6. Click **OK**. The new document opens.

To begin a new Stopframe or Keyframe animation from scratch:

Either:

- Select **New>New Stopframe Animation** from the **File** menu.
  - or -

- Select **New>New Keyframe Animation** from the **File** menu.

A new document window opens in the respective Animation mode.

To convert an existing drawing to either animation mode:

1. Choose **Convert to Stopframe Animation** or **Convert to Keyframe Animation** from the **File** menu. You'll be prompted to save changes (if any) to your existing drawing.

2. Select **Yes** to save your work, **No** to convert to an animation or **Cancel** to continue working on your current drawing.

To adjust the basic layout of your animation:

1. Choose **Page Setup** from the context toolbar (shown with Pointer or Rotate Tool selected).

2. Adjust your settings as described above.

3. Click **OK**.

> You can modify page characteristics such as page size and orientation from the Pages context toolbar.

To save an animation:

- Choose **File>Save...** DrawPlus saves animation documents in the proprietary DPA format.

Working with Stopframe animation

In Stopframe animation mode you'll be working predominantly with the Frames tab. It is ideally suited for animation because of its width and easy control of individual frames (stopframes are spread along the tab for easier management).

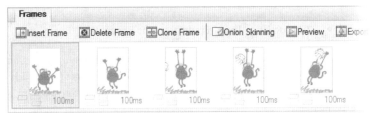

Use the Frames tab exclusively to insert, delete, clone or reorder frames, and access individual frame properties. The tab also lets you preview the animation and enable onion skinning directly; exporting as a standalone animated GIF or video is carried out via the **File** menu.

The Frames tab is designed for Stopframe animation only, and only shows while in this mode. Don't get this tab confused with the Storyboard tab, used in DrawPlus's Keyframe animation mode (see p. 230**Error! Bookmark not defined.**). Each tab hosts distinctly different tools suited to the respective animation type.

In most cases, your new Stopframe animation will have a single initial frame (e.g., Frame 1). To create new frames, you can either clone the current frame or insert a blank frame after the current frame. Choose to clone if you will be reusing the current frame's contents with a transformation of some kind (the most common way of simulating change or movement).

Once you've finished creating frames you can preview or export your animation, just as you would play the frames of a movie.

To view the Frames tab:

- Unless the tab is already displayed, click the ▬▬▲▬▬ handle at the bottom of your workspace to reveal the tab.

To clone the current frame to a new frame:

- Select a frame in the Frames tab, and choose **Clone Frame**.

The frame is added after the selected frame.

> ✱ Alternatively, use the Blend Tool to automatically create "intermediate" stopframes in steps between objects.

To generate a new blank frame:

- Choose [ ] **Insert Frame** from the Frames tab.

Any new frame appears on the Frames tab to the right of existing frames, and then becomes the current frame. If you use the Frame Manager (right-click a frame and choose **Insert...**) you can choose to add frames before/after any existing frame.

To navigate between frames:

- Click on any visible frame to display its objects on screen (objects can then be edited).
  - or -

  Click the navigation buttons on the **Hintline** toolbar to jump to start/end frame and navigate frame-by-frame.

To rename a frame:

- Right-click a frame and choose **Properties...**. In the **Name** field, type in a new frame name. The new name is shown on the Hintline toolbar.

To change frame sequence:

- Drag the selected frame to a new position in the frame order. When the dragged frame's thumbnail creates a slightly wider space between two frames than usual, release the mouse button to place the frame to be moved.

To delete a selected frame:

- Click [ ] **Delete Frame** from the Frames tab.

Onion Skinning

Onion skinning is a standard animation technique derived from cell animation, where transparent sheets enable the artist to see through to the preceding frame(s). It's useful for enabling precise registration and controlling object movement from frame to frame. You can turn the feature on or off (the default is off) as needed, and set the number of previous frames that will be visible (normally one).

To turn onion skinning on or off:

1. From the Frames tab, click the 🗹 **Onion Skinning** button to turn onion skinning on or off.

2. (Optional) 📇 To set more than one previous frame to be visible, click **Properties**, then set the number of frames in the **Onion Skinning** input box.

The preceding frame's objects will show behind those of the currently selected frame.

Previewing Stopframe animations

You can **preview** your animation prior to export at any time either directly from your Frames tab (shown in a Preview window) or from within your default web browser.

To preview in the Preview window:

- Click ▷ **Preview** on the Frames tab.

The animation loads into the Preview window and begins playing at its actual size and speed. Notice that you see only the drawn portion of the animation—any extra surrounding white space is cropped away. You can use the control buttons (Play, Stop, etc.) to review individual frames.

To preview in a web browser:

- Select **Preview in Browser** from the **File** menu. The animation loads your default web browser and begins playing.

This actually exports a temporary copy of the animation, using the current export settings and displays it in your web browser. You can leave the browser open and DrawPlus will find it again next time you issue the command.

Working with Keyframe animation

When compared with Stopframe animation (see Getting started with animation on p. 223), **Keyframe animation** offers a more powerful and efficient animation technology—it saves having to declare every frame, letting your computer do the hard work! Essentially, the technique lets you create only user-defined **keyframes** through which objects animate, with each keyframe containing **Key objects** which can be assigned a position, rotation, attributes, etc.

Intermediate steps between Key objects are created automatically and produce a smooth professional-looking inter-object transition (this is called **Tweening**); Tweened objects are created as a result. You won't see these intermediate steps showing tweened objects by default, but they exist transparently between key objects throughout your animation.

The Storyboard tab is the workspace for laying out your animation "story" in a chronological keyframe-by-keyframe sequence (from left to right). On export, your animation will play in this direction. Using the above "bee" animation in the tab illustration as an example, the bee is animated, while the sun and "Buzzzz" text remain static objects.

By adding objects (bee and sun) to a starting keyframe it's possible to automatically copy (or more correctly **run forward**) those objects forward when you create subsequent keyframes. This in itself doesn't affect animation, but it's the repositioning of a run forward object (such as the bee) in later keyframes that creates "movement."

Once keyframes are created, the animator has a great deal of control over how objects are run forward (or even backwards). You can introduce objects anywhere on the storyboard (so they appear for a limited time), and either run them forward or backwards by a specific number of keyframes (or right to the start or end of the storyboard). The "Buzzzz" text in the above example will only show from keyframes 3 onwards (i.e., from 4 seconds).

Supporting tabs

Keyframe animation mode also presents other tabs that support the Storyboard tab. These are exclusively used within keyframe animation (and do not show in normal or stopframe animation mode), i.e.

- The **Easing tab** is used for applying linear or non-linear changes between key objects with use of editable envelopes (e.g., to change object position, morph, scale, rotation, skew, colour, and transparency).

- The **Actions tab** allows objects and keyframes to be attributed actions which will run (e.g., go to a URL or designated marker) when an event is triggered (e.g., MouseOver, Rollovers, etc.).

Advanced keyframe animation

DrawPlus provides a range of features for the more experienced user, i.e.

- Apply actions in response to object events or at a specific keyframe either via an easy-to-use dialog or develop ActionScript™ code directly. Actions are great when developing interactive applications or games.

- Use the Keyframe camera for panning, zooming and rotation effects over keyframes.

- Masking lets you produce cutaways, i.e. punching through a layer(s) to reveal underlying objects.

- Add and manage sound and movies to enhance your animation. Manage files from one central location with the Media tab, which also allows viewing and direct replacement of media.

Getting started

Keyframe animations are created in a specific order:

1. Create your DrawPlus Animation file.

2. Create object(s), either static or for animation, on the page.

3. From the Storyboard tab, insert the number of keyframes and their duration via a dialog.

4. **Reposition** objects in subsequent keyframes to effect animation.

5. Export your keyframe animation as Adobe® Flash® (SWF).

To create a keyframe animation:

1. Select **Create>Keyframe Animation** on the Startup Wizard.

2. From **Page Setup**, review document types in the left-hand pane.

3. Select a document type thumbnail from a Web, Screen, or Mobile category in the left-hand pane—ideal for presentation via website (banners, adverts, etc.), as a computer presentation, or on a handheld device.

4. (Optional) In the **Paper** section at the right-hand of the dialog, swap your measurement units (e.g. to pixels), and change page size and/or orientation.

5. (Optional) In the lower **Animation** section, you can configure animation-specific settings.

6. Click **OK**.

> ✹ You can convert your existing drawing to a keyframe animation by using **File>Convert to Keyframe Animation**.

To view the Storyboard tab:

*   Unless the tab is already displayed, click the ▬▬▲▬▬ handle at the bottom of your workspace to reveal the tab.

We'll assume that you've drawn objects on the first keyframe. You can run forward these automatically throughout your animation by creation of additional keyframes—this builds up your animation "story" quickly. Other methods exist to run objects forward (and backwards) but let's concentrate on the insertion of keyframes to do this.

To insert keyframes:

1. From the Storyboard tab, select a keyframe and choose 🔲 **Insert**.

2. From the dialog, choose the **Number of keyframes** to add to the Storyboard tab. Set a default **Keyframe duration** for each created keyframe.

3. Choose to add keyframe(s) at a **Location** before or after the currently selected keyframe or before/after the first or last keyframe.

4. (Optional) Check **Insert blank keyframes** if you don't want to include run forward objects in your keyframes. Blank frames are useful "filler" frames that add breaks in your animation for messages, logos, etc.

5. Click **OK**.

An inserted frame will honour any animation runs that may transect it if the **Insert blank keyframes** setting remains unchecked (by creating an additional tweened object). If checked, the blank frame will break any transecting animation path(s) and not add tweened objects.

Once you've created a keyframe sequence you can sub-divide or split any selected keyframe further.

To split a selected keyframe:

*   Click the 🔳 **Split keyframe** button on the Storyboard tab.

*   From the dialog, enter the number of divisions that the keyframe is to be split into, then click **OK**. Each new keyframe's duration is an equal division of the original keyframe's duration.

To view or edit a particular keyframe:

*   Select a keyframe in the Storyboard tab.

To delete a keyframe:

*   Select the keyframe and choose 🔲 **Delete**.

Keyframe duration

Keyframe duration represents the amount of time in between each individual keyframe. The value is set according to how the keyframe was created, i.e.

- Inserting keyframes (blank or otherwise) lets you set the keyframe duration in an Insert Keyframes dialog (default 1 second).

- A splitting operation will create new keyframes whose duration will be a division of the selected keyframe's duration (by the number of keyframes to be split).

A keyframe's duration can be altered manually at any time.

To set the duration of an individual keyframe:

- Click the keyframe's duration (e.g., 1500ms) under its thumbnail, and, when selected, type a new value then click away.

★ The total duration of your animation is shown on your last keyframe, e.g. (5.0s).

Storyboard control

Storyboard control is possible by using a selection of buttons grouped together on the Storyboard tab (equivalent options are on the **Storyboard** menu). They operate across the entire storyboard, as opposed to on an individual keyframe or key object.

 Break storyboard — Breaks the animation run that transects through a selected keyframe into two separate runs.

⊳⊲ **Compact storyboard**	A tool for tidying up your storyboard; any keyframes containing only tweened objects are removed from the storyboard.
◻ **Scale storyboard**	Expands or shrinks the whole storyboard. All keyframe durations are automatically adjusted to fit proportionately to the new **Scale** duration.

Adding sound

To complement the visual effect of your keyframe animation it's possible to add audio. Sounds can be added either for the duration of a specific keyframe, or when an action is applied to an object event (see Applying actions on p. 242 for details on actions and events).

To add an audio clip:

1. On the Storyboard tab, click on the keyframe's 🎵 **Sound** icon (located below the frame's thumbnail).

2. From the dialog, navigate to your audio file, select it and click the **Open** button.

To remove a selected keyframe's audio clip, right-click and select **Clear Background Sound**.

Adding movies

As well as using sound in your keyframe animation, you can introduce movie clips. The movie is inserted into your chosen keyframe as an object which like any other object (QuickShape, Text, etc.) will need to be run forward for the movie to play throughout the animation.

DrawPlus supports various video formats including Flash Video (FLV), Flash SWF, AVI, WMV, and QuickTime.

To add a movie:

1. Select the keyframe to which the movie is to be added.

2. Select **Movie Clip...** from the **Insert** menu.

3. From the dialog, navigate to your movie file and select it.

4.   Click **Open**.

5.   Position the displayed ⁺▷ cursor where you want the movie to appear.

6.   Either:

•   To insert the movie at the movie's original size, simply click the mouse.

     - or -

•   To set the size of the inserted movie, drag out a region and release the mouse button.

7.   (Optional) Use the object toolbar controls to run forward/backward to the end/start of the storyboard (or by a set number of keyframes).

Previewing keyframe animations

You can **preview** your animation at any time either in a web browser or in Flash Player (This is a DrawPlus install option). This is a quick way of checking it prior to export.

To preview:

•   Click the down arrow on the ▷ ▾ button on the Storyboard tab, then choose to either:

     •   **Preview In Browser....** The option displays a dialog which lets you preview in your web browser either standalone or by loading a target HTML page and associated SWF file (the target SWF file, e.g. a WebPlus banner, will be replaced by the animation to be previewed). Check **Preview using existing HTML file** for the latter, then navigate to and select HTML and SWF files.

          - or –

     •   **Preview in Flash Player** (default). Use the navigation controls to review your animation as it would appear as an exported Flash SWF file. The animation loads Flash Player (if installed) and begins playing in a Flash Preview window.

Keyframe object control

We've just looked at storyboard control. However, a whole series of important **object control** tools are also available in keyframe animation. They are available on an **object toolbar**, displayed in-context under any selected object.

Initial grouped objects show run forward, and grouped object buttons

Objects along the animation run show buttons for conversion to key objects, and object placement and attributes buttons in both directions.

The insertion of keyframes when you begin your animation will automatically run objects forward or backward. However, **Run Forward** and **Run Backward** commands let you introduce new objects in your animation which run across a limited number of keyframes or the entire storyboard.

To run object(s) forward/backward:

1. Select the keyframe which contains your chosen object.

2. Select the object, then click ▷▷ **Run forward** (or ◁◁ **Run backward** if on a later keyframe), located on the object toolbar directly under the selected object.

3. From the dialog, choose to **Run Length** either **To end of storyboard** or by **N Keyframes** (enter a number of keyframes to copy to).

Once run forward or backward, you can move an object on any keyframe (normally the last) to make animation work. Objects that are not moved are called **tweened objects**, and show as transparent square nodes (see below; **B**) which are automatically created between any two **key objects** (**A**). If you move any of these interim tweened objects you change your animation to follow a non-linear path (see below)—as a result, the tweened object becomes a key object (**C**).

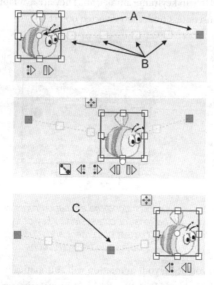

This takes care of repositioning objects, but what about changing an object's transform (morph, scale, rotation, and shear) or attribute (colour or transparency)? Simply, a selected tweened object can be modified just like any other object—it will be converted to a key object automatically as a transform or attribute change is applied.

> 🖈 　⦿ 🖾 Use **Convert to key object** to lock a tweened object into place (by making it a key object). Use the opposite command, **Convert to tweened object**, to convert back to a tweened object (removing any repositioning, transforms, or attributes local to the object). Both options are on the object toolbar.

The Object toolbar also offers two commands for repositioning objects along the storyboard. **Update placement backward** updates a previous object's position to match the selected key or tweened object's current position. Conversely, **Update placement forward** updates later object's position accordingly.

To change object placement:

1. Select the object whose positional information you want to apply forward or backward.

2. From the object's toolbar, click either:

   - ◁ **Update placement backward** to make a previous object's position match the selected object's position.
     - or -

   - ▷ **Update placement forward** to do the same to later object positions.

3. From the dialog, choose to **Run Length** either to the beginning/end of the storyboard, or to a set number of keyframes before/after the currently selected object (choose the Run length drop-down menu, pick **N Keyframes** and enter a number of keyframes).

4. Click **OK**.

Like DrawPlus's Format Painter, you can also apply a specific object's attributes (colour, transparency, filter effects, shadows, etc.) to previous or later objects.

To change object attributes

1. Select the object whose attributes you want to apply forward or backward.

2. From the object's toolbar, click either:

   - The ◁ **Update attributes backward** button to apply attributes to previous objects.
     - or -

   - The ▷ **Update attributes forward** button to apply attributes to later objects.

3. From the dialog, choose to **Run Length** either to the beginning/end of the storyboard, or to objects a set number of keyframes before/after the currently selected object (choose the Run length drop-down menu, pick **N Keyframes** and enter a number of keyframes to copy to).

4. Click **OK**.

You'll also find some useful options on the Run menu which can also be used to manipulate objects between keyframes or along the whole animation run.

Some other settings affect how objects animate along the animation run. These are hosted on the Easing tab and control object rotation, temporal tweening, natural motion, and how keyframes obey a Keyframe camera. The settings are applied between key object "segments" (and will apply until the next key object) or throughout the animation's run depending on the **Apply to Whole Run** check box setting (unchecked or checked, respectively). When the option is unchecked, objects can adopt different combinations of settings independently of each other.

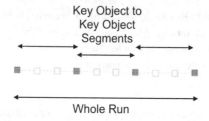

To configure a "segment", select the first Key object (■) then configure settings in the Easing tab (with Apply to Whole Run unchecked).

Clockwise Rotation	When checked, any rotation between objects is performed clockwise. Uncheck to rotate in an anti-clockwise direction.
Temporal Tween	Check to tween evenly between keyframes or over the whole storyboard (ignoring individual keyframe's time durations). Uncheck to honour any keyframe time durations. This is kept checked in most instances.
Natural Motion	When checked, animation occurs along a smoothed curving path through objects. Uncheck to animate along straight paths, with distinct "cornering" along the object's motion path.
Rotate on path	Check to allow an object (e.g., an arrow) to automatically rotate with changes of direction along an animation path. Uncheck for the object to follow the path but not to re-align to it.

Obey camera	If using the Keyframe camera feature, when the option is checked then a selected object will be panned or zoomed into. When unchecked, the object remains static, ignoring the camera. Use when text (company logo, a message, etc.) is to be permanently presented while panning and zooming is performed in the background.

Autorun

Although switched off by default, this advanced feature speeds up the animation process by automatically creating objects, their placement and attributes along the length of the storyboard, from a specific keyframe onwards. Even when editing an object, the changes are reflected throughout. Without Autorun enabled, objects are presented across keyframes by using the Insert button or clicking the object toolbar's **Run forward** or **Run backward** buttons.

> The Autorun feature does not "autorun" objects backwards but instead only runs objects forward.

To autorun objects:

1. Click ▷▷ ▾ **Autorun** on the Storyboard tab. The button is highlighted when enabled. Click again to disable.

2. Create or modify an object on a keyframe to see the effect on the object in subsequent keyframes.

As well as switching the Autorun feature on and off, you can also check one of the following options (click the down arrow on the Autorun button) to change how Autorun operates:

Creation and Placement	By default, an object will be created on every subsequent keyframe and object placement is mirrored throughout the subsequent keyframes of your storyboard.
Creation	The object is created on every subsequent keyframe throughout your storyboard but the object's position on keyframes remains unaffected.
Placement	The object's position is mirrored on subsequent keyframes on your storyboard.

Attributes	The attributes (colour, transparency, effects) of an object are mirrored to the same object on subsequent keyframes on your storyboard.

Applying actions (keyframe animation)

Selected objects can be assigned an event and corresponding **action**. The use of actions provides an interactive experience in response to a user's mouse up/down/press/release, key press/up/down, roll over, etc. As a typical example, an event such as a mouse press on an object can initiate an action such as a jump to a particular keyframe, e.g. an important point in your animation that could indicate contact details, important messages, etc.

Actions are grouped into a tree menu structure whose categories include:

- **Advanced**: Begin/End blocks, apply conditions, create variables, variable control.

- **Browser**: navigate browser to URL, navigate frame to URL, open browser with URL.

- **Effect**: named object control (hide, show, recolour).

- **Position**: move objects by pixel or to screen areas.

- **Pre-loader**: rewind animation, object stretch.

- **Sound**: increase/decrease volume, play/stop sound, set volume.

- **Timeline**: go to marker, animation frame, animation playback control (stop, play, rewind).

DrawPlus makes use of ActionScript, a language specifically designed for Adobe Flash applications, to allow a high level of interactivity between the exported Flash SWF and the user (e.g., a web visitor).

When an action is applied from the menu you may be prompted for a parameter setting (pixel width, colour, etc) but you can alter parameters at any time—without having to view underlying ActionScript code.

Optionally, a new action can be created from scratch within the dialog. Simply code directly or paste ActionScript into an Edit window.

To apply an action to selected object(s):

1. Select an object on any keyframe.

2. Double-click an event from the Actions tab.

3. From the dialog, navigate the tree menu, expanding the options if necessary, and click on a chosen action (e.g., Timeline Actions>Go to marker X).

4. Click the ⎣>⎦ button to apply the selected action (it moves across into the Applied Actions box), then repeat for optional additional actions. You may be presented with a dialog which prompts for object names or parameter values (colours, number of pixels, marker names, etc.) required for the underlying ActionScript code to act on.

5. (Optional) For multiple applied actions, you can order the Applied Actions list with the **Up** or **Down** buttons.

6. Click **OK**. You'll notice the selected event now shown in bold in the Actions tab.

The applied action can be edited by double-clicking the tab's bold event entry and, from the dialog, clicking the **Params** button (with object selected). To delete an action, use the **Delete** button to remove it.

We've looked at actions assigned to objects, but a keyframe can equally have an action associated with it. Especially useful on a starting keyframe, an Effect Action can be used to hide one or more selected objects before having them displayed on the second and subsequent keyframe (great for text introductions!). Actions are applied to keyframes via the **Frame Actions** dialog, which offers the same actions as those that can be applied to objects.

To apply action(s) to a keyframe:

*   Click on the 🔧 icon under the keyframe's thumbnail.

The dialog displayed is identical to that used for actions applied to objects. Follow the above object actions procedure to apply actions to keyframes.

ActionScript, the underlying scripting language for actions, is normally hidden from the user in the above easy-to-use dialogs—you can view actions, their settings (as parameters), and select the action but generally not the underlying code driving it. However, the more experienced and/or adventurous can make use of a simple text entry system for developing ActionScript code from the same dialog.

To create custom ActionScript:

1. For a selected object, double-click an event from the Actions tab.
   - or -

   For a keyframe, right-click the keyframe and choose **Frame Actions**.

2. Click the **New** button to add a New Action entry to the Applied Actions list.

3. With the entry selected, click the **Edit** button. The Action Script Code Editor window is displayed.

4. Enter your ActionScript code either by coding directly or by pasting existing code in the window.

5. Click **OK**.

Click the **Flatten** button to rationalize several listed actions into one. A combined action named "Flattened Code" is created instead. Each code snippet will be run consecutively.

> ActionScript Version 2 is supported in DrawPlus.

Creating markers

Working in a similar manner to bookmarks, markers work along with actions, allowing jumps to particular keyframes on the storyboard. Markers are positioned between keyframes along the storyboard and need to be activated for use. Each marker can be named, which is especially useful for marker identification when you're using multiple markers along your storyboard. Additionally, a marker can be used to stop an animation, preventing your animation from looping—the **Stops playhead** marker setting will prevent the animation from continuing past that marker position.

To set a marker:

1. Click a ▽ marker icon after a chosen keyframe.

2. From the dialog, enter an easily identifiable **Marker Name**.

3. (Optional) Check **Stops playhead** to prevent your animation from continuing.

4. Click **OK**.

5. The marker's appearance will change accordingly, i.e.

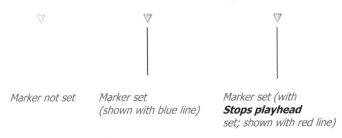

Marker not set   *Marker set*
                        (shown with blue line)

Marker set (with
Stops playhead
set; shown with red line)

When used in conjunction with the Timeline Actions "Goto marker X" or "Goto marker X and stop" the exported animation can jump to different section according to a chosen object's event or the display of a keyframe.

Affecting change over time (keyframe animation)

DrawPlus uses the term **envelopes** to describe editable motion paths (or profiles) intended to define the rate of change (acceleration/deceleration) to an object's transformation or physical attributes (colour or transparency) in your animation run.

Envelopes are applied, created, modified and saved in the Easing tab. A series of envelope types can be applied between key objects in your animation or throughout the entire animation run. Typically, a non-linear **Position envelope** would alter how an object speeds up or slows down over the animation run. Other envelope types can alter the rate of transformation such as Rotate, Morph, Scale, and Skew.

You can manually edit any profile independently of each other such that you may have a mix of edited profiles and default linear ones. The Easing tab's

Envelope type drop-down menu lets you select your envelope type, allowing you to then define a profile shape for that envelope in the pane. In most instances, an "All Envelopes" option can be used to affect a variable rate of change for **all** envelopes simultaneously.

The process or editing an envelope is identical, irrespective of envelope type. By default, any envelope is applied linearly (i.e., they change at a uniform rate over time) so you have to manually edit the envelope to apply a non-linear rate of change.

The differing rates of change of can be illustrated with a Position Envelope between two simple circles.

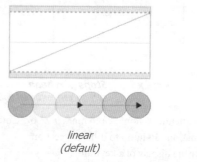 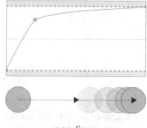

linear
(default)

non-linear
(manual editing of profile shape)

To apply an envelope:

1. Display the Easing tab.

2. Select an object from the Storyboard tab to which you want to apply the envelope.

3. Select a profile from the **Envelope type** drop-down menu (Easing tab). The displayed profile will be linear by default (see above), unless you've applied the envelope previously.

4. Pick a preset profile from the [▼] drop-
    down menu below the profile window.

    - or -

    ↖
     ∿ For a custom profile, hover over the turquoise line (the cursor
    changes) and drag in any direction to position a newly created red
    node. Repeat the process for the number of nodes that you want to add
    to make up the profile. You can then fine-tune the profile shape by
    adjusting node positions accordingly.

> ↖ Edit an existing profile from the preset drop-down menu to create
> profiles quickly.

DrawPlus will keep the applied profile unless you modify it or you reset the
profile manually. If you'll be using the profile shape in the future you can save
the current settings to your own saved profile.

To reset a selected envelope:

*   Click ⊗ **Reset**. The profile reverts to be linear (default).

To save your custom profile:

1. Modify the profile shape from an existing preset (or create from
    scratch).

2. Select **Add Easing Profile** from the Easing tab's ▷ **Tab Menu** button
    to save it. The new profile will appear at the bottom of the drop-down
    menu below the profile window.

To delete a profile preset:

1. Select **Manage Easing Profiles...** from the ▷ **Tab Menu**.

2. From the dialog, select the preset entry, click the **Delete** button, then
    click **OK**.

Exporting animations

Exporting your stopframe or keyframe animation outputs your animation to a file which can be shared or viewed, either standalone or when included as part of a web page. DrawPlus lets you export to a variety of formats as indicated below:

Export	Stopframe	Keyframe
Flash SWF	✗	✓
Flash Lite/i-Mode	✗	✓
Video	✓	✓
Image	✓	✓
Screensaver	✗	✓

Flash SWF

The **Flash SWF** (ShockWave Flash) format has fast become the format of choice for interactive vector-based graphic animation for the web. Great for creating a simple or sophisticated animated toolbar for web page navigation, it is universally supported on web browsers. The files can be easily manipulated further (scaled, etc.) within Adobe® Flash®.

To export your animation as a Flash file:

1. Choose **Export>Export as Flash SWF...** from the **File** menu.

2. From the dialog, provide a ShockWave Flash file name and folder location, and click the **Save** button. You'll see an export progress dialog appear until the Flash file is created.

Flash Lite/i-Mode

Use if you're intending to export a keyframe animation for mobile users operating mobile phones, personal organizers, and more. The format is optimized for viewing on smaller screen displays. The outputted file type is the same as that for Flash export, with a SWF file extension.

To export to Flash Lite/i-Mode:

1. Choose **Export>Export as Flash Lite/i-Mode...** from the **File** menu.

2. From the dialog, provide a ShockWave Flash file name and folder location, and click the **Save** button. You'll see an export progress dialog appear until the file is created.

Video

Exported **video** formats include:

- **QuickTime**. The QuickTime video and animation format (**MOV**) developed by Apple Computer. It can be read on many platforms, including Microsoft Windows (needs QuickTime Player) and of course on Apple computers.

- **Serif Transparent Video**. The STV format is a useful proprietary format which can export animated text and logos with transparent backgrounds. The export benefits Serif MoviePlus users who would like to use their keyframe animation as an overlay (of titles, animated characters, etc.).

- **Video for Windows**. The Windows Audio Video Interleave file (**AVI**) is ideal for playback on a Windows computer. Defined by Microsoft, it supports different types of video, audio and image sequences in sync with a mono or stereo sound track along with compression (via a wide variety of codecs). AVIs are mainly for viewing on a computer. Appropriate codecs have to be installed on the computer.

- **Windows Media audio and Video**. The **WMV** format is best supported on PCs running Windows Media Player, although some other software even on other platforms can play WMV video. WMVs are Advanced Systems Format (ASF) files that include audio, video, or both compressed with Windows Media Audio (WMA) and Windows Media Video (WMV) codecs.

To export animation as video:

1. Choose **Export>Export As Video...** from the **File** menu.

2. From the displayed dialog's Basic tab, select your chosen export type from the **File type** and **Template** drop-down list according to the type of output video format you require.

3. (Optional) Click **Match project settings** to set an approximate video frame size based on your animation project's Page size (set in Page Setup).

4. Specify a name for file in the **Filename** box, clicking **Browse** and selecting a new location if you first wish to choose an alternate drive or folder to store your file.

5. (Optional) From the dialog's Advanced tab, make a new video template with the **Copy** button, then alter more advanced settings such as video Frame size (choose Custom then set a Width and Height), Pixel aspect ratio, Frame rate, Interlacing, Codec settings, and more, depending on the format to be exported. (See Exporting video (Advanced) in DrawPlus Help for more details).

6. (Optional) Set an export **Quality**.

7. Click the **Export** button. Your project will then be composed and converted into the specified format and you will be shown a progress bar during this process.

Image

Within Stopframe animation, this option lets you create an animated GIF by default, which we'll focus on here. For keyframe animation, you can export a single keyframe as any type of image format.

The **GIF** format is ideal for web as it's universally supported by web browsers, and, as it's a multi-part format, it's capable of encoding not just one image but multiple images in the same file. A GIF animation player or web browser can display these images in sequence, in accordance with certain settings (looping, frame delay, etc.) included in the file. The result—it moves! As with single-frame GIFs, if you opt to export your animation with the Transparency setting turned on, any unfilled regions of the graphic will become transparent in the GIF. All other regions will become opaque. For details on using transparency in GIFs, see Using transparency effects on p. 170.

To export as an animated GIF:

1. Choose □ **Export** from the Frames tab.

2. The Animated GIF format is pre-selected on the **Format** drop-down menu by default; if not, select it. If you choose another format, only the current frame will be exported. For full details on GIF export options, consult Exporting objects and drawings on p. 263.

3. Set a size for the GIF animation. Leave the dpi setting at 96 for standard screen resolution.

4. On the **Animation tab**, which only appears in Stopframe Animation Mode, you can preview single frames or run the animation sequence, and make some final playback adjustments to the animation properties.

5. Click the **Export** button (or **Close** to simply record the settings if you plan to preview in a browser first).

6. Provide a file name and folder location, and click **Save**. Don't worry if you have extra white space around your image. Any unused border area will be cropped automatically, just as you saw in the Preview window.

12 Publishing and Sharing

Printing basics

DrawPlus supports printing directly to a physical desktop printer (e.g., All-in-ones, Inkjet and Laser printers) or to an electronic file such as Adobe Acrobat PDF (see p. 262). Printing your document to a desktop printer is one of the more likely operations you'll be performing in DrawPlus. The easy-to-use Print dialog presents the most commonly used options to you, with a navigable "live" Preview window to check your print output.

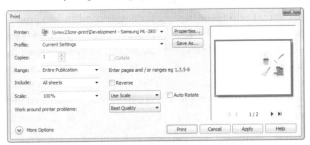

The dialog also supports additional printing options via the **More Options** button including **Double-sided Printing**, **Manual Duplex**, and many other useful printing options. One particular option, called **Layout**, allows for print-time imposition of your document—simply create a booklet or other folded document at the print stage.

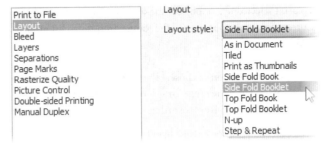

For a detailed description of each option, see Interactive Print Preview in DrawPlus Help.

> If you're working with a service bureau or commercial printer and need to provide PDF output, see Publishing as PDF on p. 262.

To set up your printer or begin printing:

1.   Click 🖶 **Print** on the **Standard** toolbar. The Print dialog appears.

2.   Select a currently installed printer from the **Printer** drop-down list. If necessary, click the **Properties** button to set up the printer for the correct page size, etc.

3.   Select a printer profile from the **Profile** drop-down list. You can just use **Current Settings** or choose a previously saved custom profile (.ppr) based on a combination of dialog settings; **Browse...** lets you navigate to any .ppr file on your computer. To save current settings, click the **Save As...** button, and provide a unique profile name. The profile is added to the drop-down list.
     Note: If you modify a profile settings, an asterisk appears next to the profile name.

4.   Select the number of copies to print, and optionally instruct the printer to **Collate** them.

5.   Select the print **Range** to be printed, e.g. the Entire Publication, Current Page, or range of pages. For specific pages or a range of pages, enter "1,3,5" or "2-5", or enter any combination of the two.

     To print selected text or objects, make your selection first, then choose Current Selection appearing in the **Range** drop-down list **after selection**.

     Whichever option you've chosen, the **Include** drop-down list lets you export all sheets in the range, or just odd or even sheets, with the option of printing in **Reverse order**.

6.   Set a percentage **Scale** which will enlarge or shrink your print output (both page and contents). A 100% scale factor creates a full size print output. Alternatively, from the adjacent drop-down list, choose **Shrink to Fit** to reduce your document's page size to the printer sheet size or **Scale to Fit** to enlarge or reduce the document page size as required.

7. Keep **Auto Rotate** checked if you want your document page to automatically rotate your printer's currently set sheet orientation. When you access the Print dialog, if page and sheet sizes do not match, you'll be prompted to adjust your printer sheet orientation automatically (or you can just ignore auto-rotation).

8. Click **Print**.

More print options

Additional print options are available from the Print dialog if you're planning to use imposition at print time (see p. 259), print double-sided, control page marks, and rasterization.

Interactive Print Preview

The **Print Preview** mode changes the screen view to display your layout without frames, guides, rulers, and other screen items. Supporting toolbars allow for a comprehensive and interactive preview of your pages before printing.

Print Preview is interactive because a main feature is to provide **print-time imposition**. Put simply, this allows you to create folded books, booklets, and more, **at the printing stage** from unfolded basic page setups. Other interactive features are also available while in Print Preview.

- Select installed printers, and choose which pages to print and how they print (to printer, file or separation).

- Add and adjust printer margins.

- Switch on/off page marks when generating professional output.

Don't forget to make the most of Print Preview's powerful **viewing controls** hosted on the View toolbar. Use zoom controls, Pan/Zoom tools, and multi-page views for detailed preview work.

To preview the printed page:

1. Choose **Print Preview** from the **File** menu. In Print Preview, your first printer sheet is displayed according to your printer's setup.

2. (Optional) Choose an installed printer from the **Printer** toolbar.

3. (Optional) Adjust printer margins from the **Margins** toolbar.

4. Review your design using the page navigation controls at the bottom of your workspace.

To print via Printer toolbar:

1. Choose which page to print via the **Print Publication** drop-down list.

2. Select **Print**.

The standard Print dialog is then displayed, where settings are carried over from Print Preview.

To cancel Print Preview mode:

- Select **Close Preview** from the top of your workspace.

Print-time imposition

During print preview, you can enable imposition of your document, choosing a mode suited to your intended printed document (book, booklet, etc.). Each mode displays different toolbar options on the context-sensitive **Imposition** toolbar.

To choose an imposition mode:

- From the **Imposition** toolbar, select an option from the **Imposition Mode** drop-down list.

As in Document	Select to print pages as they appear in your document, i.e., one page per sheet. Scaling options include: • **Shrink to fit** to reduce the page to the printer sheet size. • **Scale to fit** to adjust artwork automatically to fit neatly on the printed page, taking printer margins into account. • **Scale** to specify a custom scaling percentage. The default is 100% or normal size. To scale your work to be printed at a larger size, specify a larger value; to scale down, specify a smaller value. • If you haven't set up the document as a Small Publication, but still want to print multiple pages per sheet, try using the **Fit Many**. Note that this option ignores printer margins and doesn't change the imposition (orientation) of output pages. Ensure your page layout borders don't extend beyond the printable region.

Tiled	Even if the document isn't set up as a **poster** or **banner**, you can use tiling and scaling settings to print onto multiple sheets from a standard size page. Each section or tile is printed on a single sheet of paper, and the various tiles can then be joined to form the complete page.
	• **Scale** to print at a larger size (e.g. 300%).
	• **Tile Printable Area** to tile onto only the printable area of the sheet.
	• **Tile Overlap** to simplify arrangement of the tiles and to allow for printer margins.
Print as Thumbnails	Select to print multiple pages at a reduced size on each printed sheet, taking printer margins into account.
	• Set the number of thumbnails per sheet in the **Per Sheet** box.
	DrawPlus will print each page of the document at a reduced size, with the specified number of small pages or "thumbnails" neatly positioned on each printed sheet.
Side Fold Book	Select to paginate as a side fold book, optionally using scaling options described above.
Side Fold Booklet	Select to paginate as a side fold booklet, optionally using scaling options described above.
Top Fold Book	Select to paginate as a top fold book, optionally using scaling options described above.
Top Fold Booklet	Select to paginate as a top fold booklet, optionally using scaling options described above.
N-up/N-up Repeat	Select to paginate with multiple pages on the printer sheet, with each page repeating a configurable number of times.

- **Across** sets the number of copies across the page.

- **Down** sets the number of copies down the page.

- **Repeat** selects the number of times to repeat each page.

- **Skip** lets you omit a certain number of regions on the first sheet of paper. Skipping regions is useful if, for example, you've already peeled off several labels from a label sheet, and don't want to print on the peeled-off sections.

- **Fill Last Page** will populate the last page with your repeating region rather than just printing an almost blank page.

Step & Repeat	Select to paginate with multiple pages on the printer sheet, with each sheet containing copies of the same page only.

- **Across** sets the number of copies across the page.

- **Down** sets the number of copies down the page.

Printing books and booklets

To produce double-sided sheets, click 🖶 **Print** and use the Print dialog's Double-sided Printing or Manual Duplex options (under More Options). Ensure your printer is setup for double-sided printing or run sheets through twice, printing first the front and then the back of the sheet (reverse top and bottom between runs). The sheets can then be collated and bound at their centre to produce a booklet, with all the pages in the correct sequence.

Publishing as PDF

DrawPlus can output your drawings to PDF (Portable Document Format), a cross-platform WYSIWYG file format developed by Adobe, intended to handle documents in a device- and platform-independent manner. PDF documents are ideal for both **screen-ready** distribution and **professional** printing. In DrawPlus, ready-to-go PDF profiles are available for both uses, making PDF setup less complicated.

- **Screen-ready**. If you require screen-ready PDFs you're likely to need PDF documents which are optimized for screen use, i.e., with hyperlinks, downsampled images, document security, but without pre-press page marks, bleed, etc. Downsampling images leads to smaller documents for quicker loading.

  Profiles such as "Web - Compact" and "Web - Normal" are provided for electronic use (downsampling images to 96 and 150dpi, respectively), and are ideal for hosting PDFs on websites or other electronic distribution (email).

- **Professional**. PDF documents are suited to professional printing, i.e., when you deliver a high quality reproduction of your drawing to a print partner (normally external to your company). You'll typically require page marks, bleed, ≥300dpi images, and PDF/X-1a compatibility (for CMYK output).

  To make things simple, the professional print profile called "PDF X-1a" is provided in DrawPlus (using PDF X-1a compatibility), but you should check with your print partner if PDF/X-1, and any other settings, may be required instead. A "Press Ready" profile can also be used for documents which are not intended to be PDF/X compliant.

  With PDF/X-1a or PDF/X-1 compatibility, all your drawing's colours will be output in the CMYK colour space, and fonts you've used will be embedded. A single PDF/X file will contain all the necessary information (fonts, images, graphics, and text) your print partner requires.

🖎 DrawPlus lets you operate in a CMYK colour space from document setup to professional PDF output. This involves starting with a new drawing using a CMYK Primary colour space (p. 23).

To export your document as a PDF file (using a profile):

1. Choose **Publish as PDF...** from the **File** menu.

2. Select a profile for electronic or professional output (as described above) from the **Publish profile** drop-down list.

The dialog updates with the selected profile's new settings.

3. (Optional) Make any custom settings as required by your print partner in each tab.

4. Click **OK**.

Exporting objects and drawings

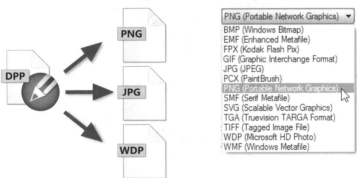

When you save a drawing, DrawPlus uses its own proprietary formats (.dpp for drawings, .dpx for templates and .dpa for animations) to store the information.

From these formats it is possible to **export** your drawing as a graphic in order to read the drawing into another application or use it on a web page. For drawings, a choice of graphics formats can be exported.

You can export at any time by using **Export as Image** or Dynamic Preview; the former lets you compare export settings, the latter allows editing during preview—great for pixel-accurate editing of your intended output!

Exporting as image

Especially if you're exporting images for the web, you can take advantage of the **Image Export** dialog, which will greatly help you in reducing file sizes and download times as far as possible while maintaining image quality. The dialog lets you export the whole page, just a selected object(s) or a user-defined region. You can also see how your image will look (and how much space it will take up) before you save it! For visual comparison, its multi-window display provides side-by-side WYSIWYG previews to compare different image formats, or the same format at differing bit depths.

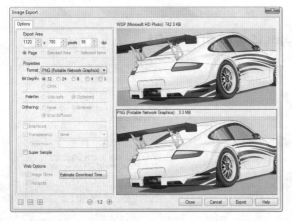

To export as an image:

1. Choose **Export>Export as Image...** from the **File** menu.

2. (Optional) From the Export Area section, you can scale the image to a new size if desired (change **pixels**), or adjust the **dpi** (dots per inch) setting. For graphics to be used on-screen, it's best to leave these values intact. The export can be based on the whole **Page**, **Selected Area** (see Defining a region for export below), or **Selected Items**.

3. From the Properties section, select the intended graphics file format from the **Format** drop-down menu. The remaining box area will display different options depending on your chosen graphics format. Change settings as appropriate to the file format selected (see DrawPlus Help for more information).

4. (Optional) From the Web Options section, you can control web elements in your image.

    *   You can uncheck **Image Slices** or **Hotspots** if you've create these elements but don't want them exported.

    *   Click the **Estimate Download Time...** button to see how long the image will take to download using various connections.

5. Click **Export**. If you click **Close**, DrawPlus remembers your preferred format and settings, particularly useful for adjusting the setting which are used if you preview the image in a browser (using **File>Preview in Browser**).

When exporting Stopframe animations, an Animation tab is shown in the dialog for frame export control.

For converting DrawPlus objects into pictures on the page, use **Tools>Convert to Bitmap...**.

For export as AutoCAD drawings, use **Export>Export for CAD/CAM** on the **File** menu.

Defining a region for export

DrawPlus lets you export a specific region in your design. The region, shown as a bounding box, is actually a layer **overlay** which can be resized, repositioned over the export area and shown/hidden. The Image Export dialog is used for the actual export process.

To define an export region:

1. From the **Standard** toolbar, click ⬙ ▾ **Overlays** and select **Export Overlay** from the drop-down menu. A bounding box is overlaid over your page.

2. Drag a corner (or edge) handle to resize the box (use the **Ctrl** key as you drag to resize the box about its centre); reposition the box over the export area.

3. (Optional) Name the Export Overlay layer in the **Export Name** box on the context toolbar (this labels the export overlay in the Layers tab and provides the default file name at export).

4. Click **Export...** shown under the box. The Image Export dialog is displayed, from which you can modify and choose an export file format (described previously).

When the overlay is applied, the bounding box is automatically selected (it shows the selection colour of the overlay layer). Clicking away from the box will deselect it (showing the box Colour), but it can be reselected at any time (e.g., for repositioning).

To select the box:

- From the **Standard** toolbar, select ⬙ ▾ **Overlays** and then **Export Overlay**.

Exporting as CMYK TIFF or JPEG

For professional printing, you can create a drawing in a CMYK colour space (p. 23), which offers colour predictability during design, processing, and output. You can either publish your design as a PDF document (p. 262) or export as image, with both options maintaining a CMYK colour space.

To export a CMYK TIFF or JPEG image:

- In the Image Export dialog, enable **CMYK**.

Dynamic preview

Although the Image Export dialog's preview options lets you see how your export will look, it's time-consuming to repeatedly export your graphic until you get the output exactly as you want it. Instead, you can use **Dynamic Preview**, which lets you swap to a **preview-and-edit** mode, showing how your graphics will export directly on the page. It also lets you edit that output while still previewing, and set up the exported file's name, format and other settings. The ability to fine-tune object positioning to pixel level, aided by a pixel grid (automatically showing at higher page magnification), is beneficial to web graphics developers.

To change export settings:

1. From the **Hintline** toolbar, click the ![icon] ▼ **Dynamic Preview** down arrow and choose **Preview Settings....** The option launches the Dynamic Preview Options dialog, which closely resembles the Image Export dialog (see above).

2. (Optional) From the Export Area section, scale the image to a new size if desired (change **pixels**), or adjust the **dpi** (dots per inch) setting.

3. Change settings in the Properties box according to your chosen **Format**. Settings change according to file type (see DrawPlus Help for more information).

4. Click **OK**.

To export via Dynamic Preview:

1. From the **Hintline** toolbar, click the  **Dynamic Preview** down arrow and choose **Export Preview As...**.

2. From the dialog, you'll be prompted for a file name to which you can save your graphic. Choose a folder location and enter a file name.

To toggle between Normal and Preview Mode:

- Click **Dynamic Preview** on the **Hintline** toolbar. The button will be enabled when in Preview mode.

To revert to Normal mode, click **Dynamic Preview** again.

While in this mode, any object can be manipulated or modified as if you are working in normal drawing mode, but what you're seeing is an accurate portrayal of your graphic to be exported.

Dynamic Preview will also automatically display a **pixel grid** at high levels of magnification. This is especially useful to web developers, who rely on pixel accuracy in their designs. As well as a visual aid, the grid can be used to accurately size objects when Snapping and Snap to Grid are enabled.

Sharing via DRAWPLUS.COM

You can share your design by print, as a distributable electronic PDF, or via the **drawplus.com** website. Publishing your design to the drawplus.com website means you can share your design and ideas with a community of like-minded designers!

The **drawplus.com** website is designed specifically as a design community. By uploading your completed design to the website, just like other DrawPlus users do, you add to the collection of published designs in the community.

The main website features include:

- **View published designs**
  To aid your design skills or to browse for fun, use the **Wall** design gallery which "showcases" public designs published by other DrawPlus users (...and yourself!). Take advantage of awesome **zoom** technology coupled with pan and zoom control. Easily view your own, the most recently uploaded, and featured designs.

- **Drawing ratings**
  Rate and comment on other people's designs—and have your own design assessed by the community!

- **Work in groups**
  Create groups of users with similar interests—great for schools, clubs, or maybe just your network designing friends. Use the **Group Wall** to view published designs in a chosen group, which can be private, public or "friends only." Post to **group forums** restricted to just group members.

- **Search**
  Find designs, groups, or other designers throughout the website.

- **Make new friends!**
  Social networking meets designing! Use **email** or user discussion
  forums to build friendships with other DrawPlus designers, especially
  those you add to your friends list. Even upload photos of yourself!

- **Profile management**
  Manage your tagline, password, timezone, language, and email
  notifications.

To share, three stages need to be carried out—register on the website, setup
account information in DrawPlus, and then upload your chosen design to the
website.

Registering for the first time

1. Click **Share** on the **Standard** toolbar.

2. Click the **Join Now!** button. You'll be taken directly to **drawplus.com**
   registration.

3. From the website's registration form, enter your personal information,
   including an email address to which an activation message will be sent.
   Use the **Help** button if needed.

4. Click **Create Account**. For account activation, you'll need to check
   your email and click on the activation message sent to you. This may
   take time depending on your ISP and connection!

   Remember your Username and Password! You'll need to re-enter
   this information into DrawPlus.

5. Registration is complete after activation. All that's now required is to
   enter your account details into your DrawPlus program (see p. 271).

If you've already registered but not added your account details, click **Share** and then the dialog's **Login** button. This takes you to your account details where you can enter details as described in the next section.

> 🖎 So you don't forget to set your user account details, you'll get a reminder to register every eight days if there are no details set. You can register on the website, then transfer your username and password over, or cancel to register later.

Setting up account details in DrawPlus

1. Select **Options** from the **Pages** context toolbar.

2. In the **Options>Upload** pane, enter your remembered **Username** and **Password**.

3. (Optional) click the **Test** button to verify that the account details are correct. If successful, a "*Username and password valid*" message is produced.

   If you've forgotten your password or you've not already registered, use the accompanying **Reset Password** and **Register** buttons. For the latter, you'll be directed to the Registration page on the website (complete the registration details and click **Create Account**).

4. (Optional) Reduce the upload **Quality** to 96dpi to speed up file transfer if your Internet connection is 56k dial-up modem (at the expense of zoom quality). Otherwise, use the default 300 dpi for broadband and all other faster Internet connections.

> 🖎 If you change your account details on the website at a later date, you'll also need to make these account changes in DrawPlus.

Uploading

Once you've successfully created your account you can upload your design, with the option of including only specific or all pages.

☑ Page 1   ☑ Page 2

To upload your design:

1. On the **Standard** toolbar, click ![icon] **Share**.

2. In the **Share** dialog, uncheck pages you don't want to upload (use the scroll bar for more than three pages).

3. (Optional) For the upload you can choose a different account to upload to—enter a different **Username** and **Password**. Otherwise, any previously used account will be remembered.

4. Click **Upload** to transfer your selected pages.

5. On upload, a progress bar indicates upload status. On completion, click **OK** to close the dialog or click **View** to immediately see your uploaded design on the website.

13 Pressure Sensitivity
and Pen Tablets

Pressure sensitivity

When painting, or drawing lines and curves, DrawPlus lets you take advantage of pressure sensitivity in a variety of ways:

- via an installed pen tablet.

- via the Pressure tab (if pen tablet is unavailable).

via a pen tablet

Your pen tablet and DrawPlus work in perfect harmony for a truly authentic drawing and painting experience, with in-built pressure sensitivity as you draw and paint. See Using pen tablets (p. 279) for more information.

via the Pressure tab

If a pen tablet is unavailable to you, DrawPlus can simulate pressure sensitivity when using your mouse (along with DrawPlus's Pressure tab).

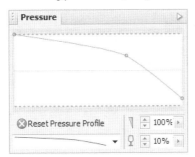

This tab is used to set pressure sensitivity globally by using a **pressure profile**. The tab lets you:

- Select a **preset pressure profile**

- Create your own **custom profile** from scratch

- Adjust how brush, pen, or pencil **width** and **transparency** changes as it responds to pressure

- Control the **maximum** and **minimum pressure**.

The pressure chart may appear a little daunting at first! It becomes a lot clearer if you imagine the chart when it is superimposed over a brush itself—it represents one half of a brush stroke along its entire length exactly. Of course, the same profile shape will be mirrored on the lower half of the stroke.

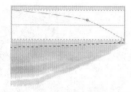

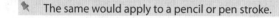
The same would apply to a pencil or pen stroke.

To apply a pressure profile:

1.   Expand the Pressure tab at the bottom right of your screen, and choose a pressure profile from the drop-down list.

The pressure chart updates to reflect the chosen profile.

2.   Apply a brush stroke or draw a line on the page. This will adopt the chosen pressure profile.

The profile is maintained until you reset it or pick another profile from the preset list.

To create a new pressure profile:

1.   Click ⊗ **Reset Pressure Profile**. This sets the pressure chart back to default.

2.   A turquoise line runs along the maximum pressure line at the top of the chart. Click on this line (the cursor changes) and drag downwards, moving the displayed red node into your chosen position. You now have a blue curve which represents the pressure profile.

3.   Repeat the process for the number of nodes that you want to add to make up the profile.

Edit an existing pressure profile from the preset drop-down menu to create profiles quickly.

You can then save the current pressure settings to your own saved pressure profile—this allows you to store and reapply your settings at any point in the future.

To save a new pressure profile:

- Click the tab's ▷ **Tab Menu** and select **Add Pressure Profile.**

Your new profile is automatically added to the bottom of the drop-down list.

To delete a pressure profile:

1. Click the tab's ▷ **Tab Menu** and select **Manage Pressure Profiles....**

2. In the dialog, select the pressure profile for deletion and click **Delete**.

Altering stroke width and opacity with pressure

For subtle pressure control, DrawPlus can vary the extent to which pen pressure can alter the width and opacity of a brush stroke or drawn line. This is expressed as a percentage of the original stroke's **Width** and **Opacity** values shown in the Brushes context toolbar (or equivalent for pen or pencil lines). Imagine the end of your stroke tapering off or getting fainter as it lifts off the page.

The width and opacity setting can be set either:

- **globally**, via the Pressure tab.

  - or -

- **per brush**, via the Stroke Brush Edit or Spray Brush Edit dialogs.

You can set the degree to which width and opacity changes either independently or in combination. Let's look at some examples... based on drawn straight line for clarity. We'll use a pressure profile (below) available from the preset drop-down menu for all examples.

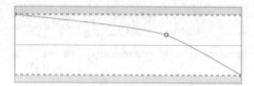

Here's how the degree of width/opacity changes the stroke's appearance.

Pressure tab	Brush Edit dialog	Result
Width: 100% / Opacity: 100%	Width: 100% Opacity: 100%	
Width: 0% / Opacity: 100%	Width: 0% Opacity: 100%	
Width: 100% / Opacity: 0%	Width: 100% Opacity: 0%	
Width: 0% / Opacity: 0%	Width: 0% Opacity: 0%	
Width: 50% / Opacity: 50%	Width: 50% Opacity: 50%	

The first example shows the default behaviour when pressure is applied.

> ★ These settings are stored independently of the currently chosen pressure profiles.

To adjust stroke width or opacity with pressure (in Pressure tab):

1. Select a previously drawn brush, freeform line, or curve.

2. In the Pressure tab, pick a pressure profile from the drop-down menu.

3. Enter a **Width** or **Opacity** value by setting a percentage value in the input box, using the slider or using the up/down arrows. The lower the value the less the pressure effects the stroke width or opacity, i.e., a value of 50% will apply half the stroke width or opacity under pressure.

For some preset brushes, stroke width and opacity are set differently to (and override) the Pressure tab's global settings. This is to more accurately represent the inherent characteristics of that particular brush. It is possible to adjust these settings further or to apply settings to a brush currently without such settings.

To adjust stroke width or opacity with pressure (per Brush):

1. Right-click on a brush in a Brush tab's category, and select **Edit...**.

2. In the Brush Properties section, check the **Initialize creation tools...** option.

3. Set **Variance** values for **Width** and **Opacity**.

4. Click **OK**. Any new stroke using the edited brush will adopt the new settings.

You can also set the pressure variance, i.e., the degree to which you apply pressure, via the Pressure tab or per brush. (See DrawPlus Help for more information.)

Using pen tablets

You can either draw or paint with your mouse or, for a more natural experience, use a pen tablet. A pen tablet is comprised of an intelligent electronic pad equipped with a pressure-sensitive pen. A rectangular "active" area responds to pressure applied by the input device (e.g., Pressure Stylus).

The pad, when connected to your computer, allows realistic sketching, freehand line drawing and painting within DrawPlus, making the drawing experience as close to a pencil or paintbrush as you can get. The tablet's pressure-sensitive capabilities in conjunction with DrawPlus allows control of stroke width or transparency when drawing or painting.

DrawPlus works equally well from entry-level to professional pen tablets from all the major tablet manufacturers including Wacom® and AipTek.

Within DrawPlus, you can use the **Pressure Studio** to calibrate your tablet's pressure response and to customize your own assignments for your tablet's ExpressKeys*, TouchStrip*, or TouchRing*. DrawPlus settings take precedence over your device's original settings.

* Not available on some pen tablets.

Using Pressure Studio

DrawPlus's Pressure Studio acts as an interface between your tablet and DrawPlus, purposely designed to:

- Calibrate pressure response (below) for multiple input devices, so that DrawPlus tools respond more predictably per device.

- Set up your tablet's key assignments from within DrawPlus (if your tablet supports function keys).

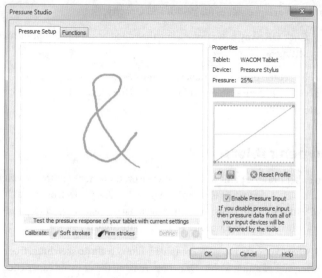

The studio offers:

- A **practice area** for automatically calibrating your tablet's input devices (Pressure Stylus, Eraser, Airbrush, etc.) by drawing soft/firm strokes. Manual calibration for fine-tuning is also possible. As you swap between each device (e.g., between pen stylus and eraser) the pressure response curve for that device is displayed accordingly.

- Management of pressure **response profiles**. Preset profiles are available to resolve common problems associated with unexpected pressure response.

- **Disabling of pressure input globally,** to allow DrawPlus to operate without tablet pressure sensitivity.

To launch Pressure Studio:

- Select 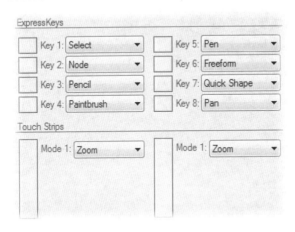 **Pressure** from the **Standard** toolbar. The **Pressure Studio** is displayed.

> Before calibration, practise drawing with your input device in the practice area!

The calibration process is described in detail in the DrawPlus Help.

Function key assignment

If your pen tablet is equipped with ExpressKeys (or equivalent), Pressure Studio lets you assign your tablet's keys to DrawPlus tools. The studio changes depending on the type of pen tablet installed, so you'll get an accurate representation of your pen tablet's key layout shown within Pressure Studio's Functions tab.

ExpressKeys

	Key 1:	Select ▼	Key 5:	Pen ▼
	Key 2:	Node ▼	Key 6:	Freeform ▼
	Key 3:	Pencil ▼	Key 7:	Quick Shape ▼
	Key 4:	Paintbrush ▼	Key 8:	Pan ▼

Touch Strips

	Mode 1: Zoom ▼	Mode 1: Zoom ▼

Example of Wacom Intuos 3's ExpressKey assignment in DrawPlus.

To customize your function keys:

1. With the Functions tab in view, select an alternative tool from the drop-down list. Pressing the appropriate key on your tablet will activate that tool in DrawPlus.

2. Click **OK**.

To revert to the tablet's default key assignment:

1. Select the "Tablet Default" option from a specific key's drop-down list.

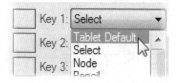

2. Click **OK**.

14 Index

Index